A.S. Panneerselvan is Executive Director of Panos South Asia and the Readers' Editor of *The Hindu*. Apart from being a regular columnist, he is also a journalism teacher and is an adjunct faculty of the prestigious Asian College of Journalism, Chennai. With wide experience in both print and television journalism, he is a board member of the Organisation of News Ombudsmen and Standards Editor representing Asia. He was a fellow of Reuters Journalism Fellowship programme at the University of Oxford in 1998.

UNCERTAIN JOURNEYS

LABOUR MIGRATION FROM SOUTH ASIA

Edited by
A.S. Panneerselvan

SPEAKING
TIGER

PANOS
SOUTH ASIA

SPEAKING TIGER PUBLISHING PVT. LTD
4381/4 Ansari Road, Daryaganj,
New Delhi–110002, India

First published by Speaking Tiger 2018

ISBN: 978-93-88326-73-5
eISBN: 978-93-88326-72-8

10 9 8 7 6 5 4 3 2 1

Typeset in Minion Pro by SÜRYA, New Delhi
Printed at Sanat Printers, Kundli, Haryana

This work was carried out with support from the Swiss Agency for
Development and Cooperation (SDC). The opinions expressed in this
book are those of the authors and do not necessarily represent the views
of SDC or Switzerland's Federal Department of Foreign Affairs.

Contents

People

Introduction: Uncertain Journeys

A.S. PANNEERSELVAN

Panos South Asia's vision is the creation of inclusive, democratic and just societies. We seek to renegotiate power through the media, by enabling the inclusion of diverse opinions, ideas and theories in the debates on governance and development. To realize this vision, we work through an innovative understanding of media dynamics and aim to create an enduring partnership with the media to widen the public sphere.

Panos South Asia (PSA) has evolved a roadmap with five clear signposts to reach its ambitious destination. One, the media in South Asia is our primary area of focus. Two, we have made gender an integral part of all our activities. Three, we seek to create democratic spaces in media discourse through interventions at multiple levels: by providing young journalists training in honing professional skills, both content and technical; by providing fellowships to mid-career journalists who have spent considerable time in the profession but have very little time or opportunity to investigate critical issues, thus enabling them to undertake their desired work; and lastly, but crucially, through intervention with media owners, proprietors and editors—the gatekeepers who decide media content. Four, PSA consciously works with four different platforms: print, radio, television and new media. And finally, we focus only on five broad themes: conflict, environment, public health, globalization and media development.

*

A major area of concern for Panos South Asia has been the impact of globalization on labour, and its attendant problems, including migration and remittances. In 2013, we asked Prof. D. Narashima Reddy and Prof. J. Jeyaranjan to produce a monograph, 'Globalisation and Labour in South Asia.' This monograph became the impetus for us to look into the entire universe of labour and migration in South Asia.

Reddy and Jeyaranjan documented how globalization increased international migration from South Asia to the rest of the world, particularly the Middle East, Europe and North America. The major surge in international migration from South Asia for employment and better earnings was preceded by the advent of globalization. It was largely propelled by the oil boom and the migration destinations were mostly in the Middle East. As the process of globalization continued, growing demand in the developed countries, particularly North America and Europe, for labour with better skills, brought about a surge in the migration of educated labour to the more developed countries.

There are differences across the South Asian countries when it comes to migrant destinations. For India and Pakistan, although Asia, particularly the Middle East, is still a major destination, more than one-fourth of emigrants from these two countries are in other regions. For Pakistan, Europe turns out to be a second major destination, with 16.4 per cent of its emigrant stock, and North America takes the third place with 9.1 per cent of Pakistanis there. For India, it is quite the reverse. North America is the second major destination, with 15.0 per cent of the Indian emigrant stock, and Europe takes third place with 9.7 per cent. For both Nepal and Bangladesh, the Middle East remains the primary destination, though the latter has 4.7 per cent moving to Europe. Sri Lanka has been a difficult country to categorize in terms of migration, because it was nearly impossible to separate the civil war-induced movement of people from regular labour migration over the past decade. It was while working on this issue that we felt that these macro studies—which provide the aggregate numbers and give the larger picture—needed a human face.

In 2015, Panos South Asia in partnership with the Swiss Agency for Development and Cooperation (SDC), launched a two-year Regional Project on South Asian Migrant Labour with the aim of building the capacity of media in South Asia to advocate and influence regional cooperation for migrant labour. The PSA-led media initiative explored various aspects related to labour migration through on-the-ground reporting and well-researched stories in both labour-sending and destination countries. These appeared in print, and were broadcast on TV, radio and online. After two years (2015–16), it was evident that this project should be reworked to include senior journalists, in order to address the gaps and challenges experienced in the first two years and to ensure more long-term output. The SDC enthusiastically supported the idea.

In the current phase, PSA selected fifteen senior journalists from across South Asia for a fellowship that enabled them to carry out in-depth research on aspects of labour migration from the region. The fellows chose different destination countries to research, including Malaysia, Singapore, Kuwait, the United Arab Emirates (UAE), Oman and Qatar.

The function of a journalist is to perform four core tasks: verification, sense-making (analysis, interpretation, opinion), bearing witness and investigation. Bearing witness is not a passive activity. It involves a range of journalistic skills: documenting the environment where the subject of the story lives; posing the right questions to elicit relevant information; having the patience to listen, the acumen to spot contradictions in claims, and the perseverance to verify the facts. The fellowship, which involved extensive research at the home country as well as field research in destination countries, gave these reporters abundant time and space to perform the four core tasks.

The fellowship produced more than 200 articles and broadcast stories, across thirty-four media outlets, and in seven languages— English, Urdu, Nepali, Bangla, Arabic, French and Malayalam. While the broadcast fellows produced short (thirty-minute) documentaries, the print journalists distilled their eighteen months

of experience covering labour migration into long-form reportage—
brought together into this anthology. Our original plan was to have
twelve essays, but we have had to settle for eleven as one of our
fellows from Bangladesh had health problems.

*

The essays in this volume fall into three broad categories: People,
Places and Policies. Some lie at the intersections of these categories,
but ask fundamental questions about the nature and costs of labour
migration. For instance, Porimol Palma looks closely at the daily
life of Bangladeshi migrants in Singapore and asks: can human
beings be reduced to a commodity within the global free flow of
capital and business models? Rejimon Kuttapan, who has been a
journalist in West Asia for decades, wonders whether, in tracing
the difficulties faced by migrant workers in GCC countries, he is
documenting modern-day slavery. One of our fellows has opted
to use a pseudonym despite long experience in the profession—an
indication of the sensitivities involved in the chosen topic: the gap
between the liberal, progressive image that the UAE projects, and
the stark conditions and inescapable surveillance under which its
migrant workers live and work.

Other essays probe the gap between the dreams and reality faced
by migrant workers, through the lens of policy. Upasana Khadka
explores the culturally fatalistic view that migration is a lottery, with
the potential to reap good harvests, but at enormous risk. Her essay
stresses that policy changes should negate, or at least reduce, the
unknown risks of migration. A fellow journalist from Nepal, Janak
Sapkota, masterfully unravels how weak regulatory frameworks
enable agents and recruiters to convert bona-fide labour migration
for employment into human trafficking. Sabrina Toppa explores the
lives of Pakistani migrants facing death sentences in the destination
countries, alongside the government of Pakistan's lack of action
on their behalf. Policy makers must also consider the importance
of those workers who return, willingly or not, after attempting
to migrate. R.K. Radhakrishnan meticulously documents the

lives—and deaths—of migrants who return to India, including the disquieting fact that most returnees think that exile and migration is a better alternative to their current condition. Haniya Javed lays bare the irony of Pakistani migrants' fascination for Saudi Arabia: it is the most-preferred destination, but also the country from where the largest number of Pakistani workers are being deported, and in steadily increasing numbers.

David Halberstam, a 1964 Pulitzer Prize winner, explained the value of providing context for a story. He urged journalists to be creative in order to make stories important, and to provide a sense of context in order to make sure that the stories are remembered. These essays document the price people pay to earn a dignified livelihood, as well as the joy and pain of distance employment. They have context as their core element, and hence, help us to understand the labour migrant from South Asia as a human being, and not a mere remittance machine for the family or a precious foreign-exchange earner for the home country. Thulasi Muttulingam's heart-wrenching essay places the gender dynamics of labour migration from Sri Lanka in the context of decades of civil war: the high proportion of war widows and other vulnerable women in its aftermath has changed the face of migration from the country. Amantha Perera argues that poverty in Sri Lanka is accentuated by two factors—ethnic strife and climate change—forcing people to migrate for their bare livelihood. Kesang Tseten's film, *In Search of the Riyal*, moved me to tears when I first saw it, a decade ago. His latest film, *Migrant Journeys*, traces the lives of four migrant workers from Nepal who were featured in his earlier films. His essay is about two important elements: empathy in film-making and the experience of documenting the multitudinous realities in the lives of those who attempt to make it in a new country.

I am acutely aware of the range of issues covered in this anthology: the differences in the lived experiences across countries, the impact of returning and readjustment, the nuances of policy-making and its far-reaching impact and, always, the hopes, fears and dreams of the individual migrants. This realization of multiple possibilities, that dreams are alive despite numerous assaults on basic humanity, the overwhelming desire to live while existing, deters me from presenting a singular overarching interpretation of the findings of these intrepid reporters. The fact is that the subject—labour migration from South Asia—is complex, whether intellectually, emotionally or politically, and only a nuanced, inclusive, multifaceted approach can do it justice. I hope this volume adds to our understanding of the difficulties faced by the millions of men and women who step out of their own countries in search of livelihood.

Chennai
November 2018

PLACES

Liberal Mirage

NILA KUMAR

Art lovers and tourists move slowly across the sprawling halls of the Louvre museum, Abu Dhabi, stopping to look at a Renaissance painting here, an antique terracotta pot there. They walk as if in a dream, admiring both the art on display and the ingenious building. On Saadiyat island, in the heart of Abu Dhabi's US$27-million cultural district project, the iconic museum built by Pritzker-prize-winning French architect Jean Nouvel seeks to recreate the United Arab Emirates' essence. Sunlight streams in sharply through the lacy dome. Wide stretches of undulating space evoke the endlessness of a desert. The meticulously curated collections from civilizations across time and geography illustrate not only universal diversity, but also the UAE's specific place in ancient and contemporary human history.

In one of the rooms stands a life-sized Greek nude. Two teen girls in black burkhas stand in front of it, mesmerized. They look at the shapely calves and sleek arms sculpted from black marble, the painstakingly carved folds of the single piece of cloth worn on the torso, the crown of leaves on the curly hair, the casual stance of authority—it is a classic nude, a symbol of openness, confidence and power, loaned from the Louvre in Paris. Suddenly, one of the girls giggles unstoppably, and the other clicks a picture on her phone. One of them points to the source of their mirth: a fig leaf made of the same marble, with the same attention to detail, placed strategically for a modest viewing of the naked male body. The museum staff later told me that this addition was made to all the nude sculptures on display, to abide by Islamic conventions in the UAE.

The impressive Louvre is an expression of the UAE's desire to be seen as global, but a conservative core does become visible occasionally. The Emirates pride themselves on making up the most modern, cosmopolitan and West-friendly country in the Middle East. Dubai, with its skyscrapers, silken highways and unapologetic luxuries, has been a sort of El Dorado for people across the world. Never-ending construction and trade in oil-rich Abu Dhabi and Sharjah have enticed tourists, labourers, artists and engineers alike. But the UAE's aspirational image as a global economic powerhouse also makes it enormously prickly about the grittier realities that exist alongside, like stark inequalities and the attendant labour rights violations. Like the fig leaf on the sculpture, the UAE's modernity serves as a cover for the ugly truths it wants to hide.

The UAE has the largest number of migrants in the world. Over 88 per cent of its population of 9,000,000 are foreigners, most working on temporary employment contracts in white-collar, blue-collar and service industry jobs. In downtown Dubai, or in its malls and markets, it is possible to get by while speaking Hindi, Bengali, Tagalog or Urdu; an Arabic speaker may in fact find himself at a loss. Despite this overwhelming migrant presence, the UAE has granted citizenship to only a handful of migrants since it gained independence in 1971. Labour is the country's biggest resource and nearly all of it is foreign, but the profits earned and the infrastructure built by that labour are deployed for nationals first. For instance, Emiratis hold nearly 79 per cent of government jobs, despite 73 per cent of the jobs in the private sector being held by foreigners.

Many foreigners who choose employment and a non-taxable income here are aware of what they are getting into: Emirati national interest outweighs the rights, dignity and safety of individual employees, from top management to a contractual sweeper. Danish Hussain,* a leading Indian-origin businessman in Abu Dhabi, has lived here for thirty-five years, running a successful trading firm, and raising his three children. Yet, he says, 'The UAE takes care of

---

*Name changed at his request.

its own first. Welfare of foreigners is expected to come from the opportunity that the UAE creates for you, by allowing you to earn here tax-free. Everyone who comes here to work knows that they are second priority. It's something you learn to live with.' He requested anonymity because even marginal criticism of the Emirates could 'land him in trouble'.

Within days in the UAE, it's easy to observe the stratified lives of locals and migrants, and further, the hierarchy of dignity among migrants from different nations. A group of taxi drivers on a tea break at a Malayali-run snack shop in Dubai laugh when asked if all migrants face the same discrimination. 'Wages, jobs and treatment all depend on where you're from,' says Solomon, a Ugandan driver. Around him sit Pakhtun, Bangladeshi, Malayali, Sri Lankan Tamil, Ugandan and Egyptian drivers and mall supervisors ranging from twenty-five to fifty in age. Together, almost as a game, they rank nationalities by status in the UAE. 'White on top,' says a Bangladeshi—everyone agrees that that is a no-brainer. Caucasian Europeans and Americans are paid more than others for the same white-collar jobs. Then, in decreasing order of respect and pay—or 'increasing order of racism,' as the Ugandan driver put it—the group lists Arabs from other countries like Egypt and Morocco, Filipinos, Indians and Pakistanis, Sri Lankans, Bangladeshis, and finally, blacks from African countries. Conditions for non-nationals get worse the lower one goes down the food chain.

'You learn to live with it,' an Indian taxi driver from Kerala echoes Hussain's words. 'But when even something small goes wrong, the suffering is unbearable.' When Emirati passengers walk off without paying their taxi fare, for instance—every driver admits this is a common occurrence—the drivers just pay the employer the lost fare from their own pockets. All of them also work fourteen to eighteen hours a day, seven days a week, to meet their employers' revenue targets[1]. 'If I try to file a police complaint, I'll just be harassed for speaking up,' one says.[2]

The Emirates widely exploits workers, but also covers it up more aggressively than any other Arab nation. 'Labour is commodified here, and migrants are both the commodity and the consumers,' says Anuradha Mallimoggala, an Indian-origin lawyer in Dubai who has represented workers alleging abuse and non-payment, as well as defended employers in other cases. She explains that courts do penalize employers or recruiters who don't comply with labour laws, and employers can face hefty fines and jail terms. 'But the process is expensive, and unpaid workers or those who quit and have lost visas can hardly be fighting cases without a salary and a valid visa status,' she says. 'This land of opportunity has double standards, what to do?' she concludes with a shrug.

A report by Human Rights Watch (HRW),[3] documents how the kafala system and lack of labour law protections in the UAE leave migrant workers vulnerable to abuse. HRW interviewed ninety-nine workers, as well as several lawyers and recruitment agencies for this report. Researchers also sent letters with questions to fifteen UAE ministries and government bodies several times, but received no response. 'The UAE is often loath to interact with international agencies,' says Rothna Begum, the report's author and women's rights researcher for Middle East and North Africa at Human Rights Watch.

International labour-rights activists single out the otherwise progressive UAE government as one of the toughest to collaborate with on policy making. The country is intensely sovereign and prefers to constitute domestic committees—these are often opaque and have no accountability. 'The UAE might be socially liberal, but it is economically exploitative and dangerously defensive,' says a senior bishop based in the UAE, who has set up Samaritan networks in two other Gulf countries but hit a wall here. Social workers and lawyers in the Emirates say they must work entirely undercover, because the image-conscious country aggressively attempts to silence its critics.

As late as 2017, the country reformed its labour laws to tackle some chronic violations. It stipulated working conditions, kickstarted a centralized complaints mechanism, and moved towards a more skilled workforce. Officials in the Ministry of Human Resources said this was done to help boost its progressive image—essential for tourism and foreign investment—but also to differentiate the UAE from its more 'regressive' neighbours like Saudi Arabia, Oman and Qatar. Clearly, the solutions are inspired not by a fundamental recognition of human rights or need for equality, but by the urgency to buff a tarnished reputation. It's no wonder, then, that the reforms have stopped short of addressing the most entrenched labour problems: abysmal pay, employer impunity and near-enslavement under kafala visas. While even Saudi Arabia— one of the worst labour rights violators in the Middle East—has announced a statutory minimum wage for workers, the UAE has refused to set one. Worse, it justifies this by citing the need for a 'flexible labour market'.

The UAE is often represented by a two-dimensional image; the glitz and the grime seem to exist in parallel, two truths never really meeting. The more complex reality, however, is that they are tightly entwined. The greater the mirage of modernity, the higher the stakes are in preserving it. This has produced in the UAE a belligerent defensiveness, which blocks its path towards becoming the liberal state it says it wants to be.

*

Julia,* a thirty-five-year-old American primary school teacher living with her architect husband in Abu Dhabi for eight years, has been to the Louvre once. 'Only the UAE can pull something like this off. They have the wealth, of course, but they are [also] committed to being world class,' she says, using a well-worn phrase in these parts. Walking on to her balcony one Friday evening, Julia points to the bright lights along the upmarket creek. 'My favourite place down there serves unbelievable cocktails,' she says. 'Abu Dhabi is beautiful, and on most days, I feel totally free here.'

As we speak, Julia's two-year-old son is playing on the floor, lining his toys up in a train. He looks up, and asks for a snack. 'He can smell something baking,' says Julia, smiling. Annie,† her Sri

---

*Name changed at her request.

†Name changed at her request.

Lankan cook and house help, enters the room and quietly serves all of us home-baked cookies.

'When I came from Seattle with my husband, we were determined not to hire servants,' says Julia. 'But after we got pregnant, and I got my teaching job, we had to get full-time help.' Annie has worked in the household since Julia's son was two months old. 'My American guilt about hiring house help disappeared in months! It is impossible to imagine these conveniences back home, at this price.'

Julia is not comfortable with me interviewing Annie. She says she pays her ample wages and funds her medical insurance, as per law, but is aware of the fragility of her cook's life. Part of 'a Good Samaritan group' (as social workers must call themselves to avoid government scrutiny) in her Abu Dhabi church, Julia has helped raise funds for the medical and legal expenses of at least forty abused migrant workers in two years. 'I never believed the horror stories earlier, but when you meet woman after woman with bruises or unpaid wages, you start understanding that the same system that makes my life easier is actually broken.'

Several members of Julia's church group—teachers, accountants, and medical professionals from the USA, UK, Singapore and India—narrate similar experiences. All of them employ multiple workers for gardening, childcare, elder care, cooking, and cleaning. 'It is a life you just ease into, but until one of my maids confided in me about being abused at her previous workplace, I thought these were just tall stories made up by the media,' says a British paediatrician who works in a public hospital in the UAE. At first, he admits, he assumed that 'only Emirati families abused their maids', because 'they were racist about brown and black people'.

But over time, he realized that non-Emiratis abused their workers too, and that racism was not the only phenomenon that produced abuse. The entire ecosystem enables the exploitation of blue-collar workers—the employment laws, the contracts, the police system, the courts, the surveillance, 'even self-censorship by people like me.' The paediatrician offers an example: 'My boss will never keep my passport—he follows the law because he will be blacklisted if I, a

British expat, decide to complain. But I can take away my Sri Lankan maid's passport. I'll never get into any trouble for it.'

One of the most quoted examples of the UAE's progressiveness towards migrant workers is that, unlike in Saudi Arabia, employees need not obtain a no-objection-certificate (NOC) from their employers before they go home. From 2002, the UAE also banned employers from holding the workers' passports. 'We don't have to get an NOC in Dubai, that's true,' says thirty-year-old Amarjeet, a Punjabi migrant who works for a house-cleaning agency in Dubai, and has earlier worked in Jeddah, Saudi Arabia. 'But my employer still keeps the passports of the more than 100 people he employs— that's a way to prevent us from leaving.' Amarjeet knows this is illegal, and that by law, his employer can be jailed or fined 20,000 dhirams (US$ 5,445) for confiscating passports.[4] But he didn't see a way he could complain without losing his job, and thus, his visa.

On paper, the laws in the UAE say workers must be paid through electronic transfer, and that companies can be fined and blacklisted for unpaid wages. But the Labour Ministry's resources are too meagre in the face of the number of violations it must address. Amarjeet, for instance, has not been paid for three months. 'If I ask any questions, my boss will say, chal hat (get lost), and just hire a more desperate fellow on his terms. It's not as if the police will help me, or that I can go to the labour courts without knowing Arabic.'

Without passports, and under constant pressure from employers, workers do erupt in protest, especially at construction sites, or labour housing complexes. They protest hushed up deaths at work, unpaid wages and abuse. But these protests often end in arrests or mass job terminations, leading the worker to immediately lose his work visa, and be trapped in the country without legal representation, without his passport, and without enough savings or wages to go home. Many then go into hiding, working illegally. To deal with tens of thousands of such workers,[5] the UAE, like other Gulf countries, offers limited-time amnesties to 'illegal immigrants' or 'overstayers', writing off their fines, and getting their respective country's embassies to fund their journeys home.

A worrying number of migrants break under the pressure of long work hours, financial strain and the absence of dignity. In 2017, 116 Indians committed suicide, just one less than in Saudi Arabia during the same year. Up to 10 June 2018, fifty-five have already taken their own lives.[6]

These dismal conditions get worse for the most marginalized. Whatever meagre protections the UAE's labour law offers, they did not extend to one of the largest groups of migrants in the country—domestic workers—until as recently as February 2017.

*

There are over 750,000 domestic workers in the UAE, and over 65 per cent are based in Dubai, Abu Dhabi and Sharjah. Unlike other sectors, the demand for domestic workers has been robust, despite economic downturns. In the past ten years, the GCC's migrant domestic work sector has been growing at an annual average of 8.7 per cent. In Dubai and Abu Dhabi, it is growing at 8.8 per cent annually. It's not uncommon for a household to hire several domestic employees to clean, cook, drive, guard, tutor and garden.

Domestic workers, three-fourths of whom are women in the UAE, are usually attached as 'live-in maids' to a particular employer household that sponsors their visa—this is the much-criticized kafala system in the GCC. Migrant men do domestic work too, as gardeners, caretakers, pet keepers or personal chauffeurs. Living isolated in a household with limited mobility and no community, these workers, especially the women, are vulnerable to abuse. Under kafala, the practice is for the employer to keep the employee's passport and control her movement. Quitting a bad boss means losing your work visa. So, many workers from low-income countries endure a lot of abuse for a long time before running away. As soon as she leaves her employer, the worker's status becomes illegal and she can be arrested or deported. In other words, escaping abuse makes the worker illegal. On paper, the worker can file a criminal complaint against the employer, or approach labour courts—but often, she is unaware of, or unable to access the existing labour protections and rights. She is usually petrified of approaching the police stations or courts, fearing arrest and imprisonment.

After decades of criticism and campaigning around labour rights violations, there is today a marked shift in the region towards building better policies for domestic workers. 'In the last five years, five of the six GCC countries have started to adopt laws for the protection of migrant domestic workers for the very first time,' says HRW's Rothna Begum. Legal and institutional reforms have been announced in the domestic work sector in Bahrain (in 2012 and 2017), Saudi Arabia (in 2013), Kuwait (in 2015 and 2018), and in Qatar and the UAE (in 2017).

These reforms look to regulate and standardize contracts, mandate better living conditions, formalize recruitment, and plan rehabilitation and legal redress for abused workers. 'The GCC countries have for long cultivated the image of being luxurious economies meant for the good life,' says Begum. 'This image is hard to maintain as labour exploitation comes to light. So, while they try to shut down any reporting that exposes violations, they have also been forced to address some issues.'

The UAE's new reforms are motivated by the Gulf oil crisis, competition with neighbour Qatar, and its desire to be seen as the most progressive GCC country. It has had a draft law on domestic work since 2012, but only passed it in 2017, after Kuwait published its law. This royal decree includes: a regular weekly day off, daily rest of at least twelve hours, access to a mobile phone, thirty days of paid annual leave, and the right to retain personal documents like passports. Most importantly, it moves domestic work from under the purview of the Interior Ministry to the Human Resources (Labour) Ministry—a long-standing demand from rights advocates. In addition, for the first time in the GCC, the UAE allows inspection of the work premises after securing a warrant from the prosecutor. This is hugely significant, because unlike hotels or construction sites, the biggest obstacle to enforcing labour protection in domestic work was the inability to monitor the workspace of a cleaner or a cook—a private home.

Froilan Malit, a former consultant with the Ministry of Human Resources in the UAE, and the son of a Filipino migrant worker, co-authored a 2016 report for the International Organization for Migration[7] that found that the lack of bilateral labour agreements and government policies led to asymmetric information and fewer avenues to protect workers in the kafala system. To address this gap, Malit explains that the UAE is innovating recruitment processes. It has issued licenses for forty Tadbeer Service Centres. They will replace recruitment agencies by the end of 2018. Employers' requests for domestic workers will have to be routed through these centres, run by licensed private agents but supervised by the Ministry of Human Resources. The centres have accommodation for workers, and can also sponsor a few hundred workers' visas, both freeing the workers to do part-time jobs, and catering to the growing need among UAE nationals and expats for legal part-timers.

Khalil Ebrahim Khouri, assistant undersecretary for domestic workers' affairs, said Tadbeer Centres help make the hiring of domestic workers easier and cheaper and that the workers' salaries will be revised every six months. B.L. Surendranath, General Secretary of the Immigration Protection Centre, Hyderabad, India, visited some of these centres in Dubai earlier this year, on the invitation of the UAE's Ministry of Human Resources. 'I was pleasantly surprised at the well-thought out ideas at the model Tadbeer Centre,' he said.

However, some of the most fundamental matters are still unaddressed. Tadbeer Centres do not check unpaid, unequal and abysmally low wages. They do not identify or blacklist abusive employers, who can therefore keep hiring new workers. They do not remove the kafala visa sponsorship system, which is the way full-time workers will still be hired.

Unlike Kuwait, Qatar and Saudi Arabia, the UAE has still not stipulated minimum wages. 'The UAE's wage policies enable a flexible labour market that creates thousands of new jobs annually,' said the UAE's Ministry of Human Resources and Emiratisation, on

3 April 2018, justifying why it didn't believe in fixing a minimum wage.

*

The consequences of the systemic bias against domestic workers in the UAE are starkly apparent in an area like Deira, in downtown Dubai, a hub for migrant workers in various levels of conflict with the state.

The elevator of a typical fifteen-storey apartment building in Deira is packed to over its capacity, but no one offers to step out. 'Everyone is equally tired after a whole day's work, so no one wants to take the stairs,' says thirty-one-year-old Jahanara, as she drags her feet up the steps. Sixty-year-old Ratna joins her.

Jahanara is a Bengali-speaking single woman from north Bangladesh, while Ratna is a Telugu-speaking grandmother of eight from Mumbai, India. The younger woman cleans four houses a day, and cooks dinner for a fifth, while the older woman gives traditional oil massages to infants and their mothers every week. Though three decades apart in age, and from wildly different backgrounds, they have been neighbours and friends for over three years.

'It's like I found family here in this strange land,' says Jahanara, who left home six years ago to work in the Gulf, as migrants from Asia call the Middle East. She has gone home only once since, when she ran away from abusive employers in Jeddah, Saudi Arabia, and the police deported her. She returned to the Gulf soon afterwards, to Abu Dhabi this time, with a full-time job as a cook, but here too, she was cheated. 'I was promised 800 dirhams (US$218), but was paid 400 dirhams (US$109),' she says. She had to be on her feet for twelve to sixteen hours a day, eat leftovers and sleep on the kitchen floor. After enduring it for over a year, Jahanara scaled the gate one night, and escaped. 'A Pakistani taxi driver dropped me in Deira, and introduced me to Ratna.'

Ratna, who was a regular masseur in nearly eight houses in Dubai at the time, gave the nervous young woman a meal of rice, dal and—as Jahanara still recalls—'a beautiful fish fry.' She arranged for Jahanara to rent a half-room in the same apartment, and in a week, fixed part-time housekeeping work for her in the homes of an Indian and a French expat family. Each employer pays 500 dirhams (US\$136) a month. 'You earn at least three times more if you're khalli walli,' explains Ratna, using the colloquial Arabic term for undocumented or freelance migrant worker. 'You get to sleep in your own house, you get paid on time, and if your employer misbehaves, you can find a new one.'

By working for twenty-three years in Dubai and Muscat, Ratna has funded the education of her three children, the construction of a house in a Mumbai slum and the weddings of two daughters. She uses the word 'normal' while referring to being overworked, underpaid, and trading away dignity abroad for the survival of family back home. It's all part of a marginal existence as a maid in one of the shiniest economies in the world.

As Ratna puts it: 'The Gulf needs us, but like a bad husband, it also exploits us.' When they describe their lives, migrant women workers repeatedly weigh the possibility of financial empowerment against inadequate wages, routine abuse and vulnerability. It's common to be cheated by agents and traffickers, acquire debts to pay recruitment fees and get stuck in a cycle of bad employers.

To these women, changes in the law have meant nothing. The protection of domestic workers remains problematic because the UAE continues to have some form of the kafala sponsorship system, which grants employers and the government an inordinate amount of power over the worker's ability to change jobs or return home. M. Bheem Reddy of the Hyderabad-based Migrant Rights Council says the UAE's attempt to tackle kafala by allowing Tadbeer Centre agents to sponsor visas does not work, as agents are not held accountable, even if they repeatedly send different workers to the same abusive employer. 'The UAE might be better than before in trying to help migrant workers, but locals are first priority, even if they commit crimes,' says Reddy. 'None of the laws penalize employers of domestic workers for labour rights violations.'

Dhaka-based migrant rights activist Shakirul Islam, from

Ovibashi Karmi Unnayan Programme (OKUP), welcomes legal reforms, but is also circumspect. 'Most Gulf-working women who return to Bangladesh say that the revised laws have no impact on their lives,' he says. 'My understanding is that on the one hand, the employers are not aware of the law. On the other hand, they do not care about it.'

For now, it seems that the women working on the margins of one of the richest economies in the world will remain vulnerable to abuse and exploitation from their employers. And, as long as opportunities exist for them in the Gulf that they can't find at home, thousands will come to fulfil the demand for domestic and care work, knowing they could be risking everything for little or no return. These women get on flights to the UAE with their fingers crossed. As Jahanara says, 'You focus on the success stories you hear of, and hope you'll have that luck.'

*

One summer evening in Deira, word spreads among the migrant workers that two social workers and a lawyer have come to someone's house. Within an hour, nearly twenty-five domestic workers fill the small two-bedroom flat. 'We can listen to everyone's problems,' says one social worker apologetically. 'But please understand that since we work without pay, we can only take up some.' She first announces that she speaks Urdu, and her colleague, Tamil. The lawyer speaks Telugu and a smattering of Hindi. The migrants who speak these languages come forward one by one. Most of them are on expired or lapsed visas because they escaped abusive employers. Some ask how to recover the unpaid wages from former employers; others request help with ongoing cases in the labour court. The consultation goes on over kabab rolls for a quick working dinner, and several cups of lemon tea.

The social workers and the lawyer are able to leave only at midnight, rubbing their tired eyes. 'We go to meet one, and there's always hundreds,' says the lawyer. 'The issues are often the same— work visa, beatings, less than promised salary.'

When I ask if there aren't more pro bono lawyers or NGOs to aid distraught workers, the trio laugh wryly. 'If there is anybody the government hates more than a complaining worker, it is an activist helping the complaining worker,' says the social worker.

Activists, social workers, journalists, lawyers and labour-rights researchers attempting to help struggling workers in the UAE take great risks. In buzzing, cosmopolitan Dubai and Abu Dhabi, it is possible to imagine living and moving about freely. But if any of these actions involve even a mild criticism of the UAE government, the consequences are swift and strong.

No country in the region—and perhaps the world, barring Israel and China—has invested as much as the UAE on surveillance technology. After the Arab Spring in the Middle East, when social media and the internet played a pivotal revolutionary role, several countries became wary of its potential for aiding dissent. Since 2011, Gulf rulers have tightened their control over information and communication technologies. They have passed draconian legislations that effectively outlaw criticism of their regimes.

The Arab Spring was a turning point for the UAE too. In November 2012, the UAE's Emirati president, Sheikh Khalifa Bin Zayed, approved a cybercrime law that has become a tool of authoritarian control. Its vaguely worded provisions effectively criminalize the use of information technology to comment on politics and policy, to criticize senior officials or to organize demonstrations. Using the law, Emirati authorities have cracked down, most of all, on journalists and labour-rights activists. Government critics, bloggers and human-rights defenders have been detained or are disappearing at an alarming rate as a result of their social media activity, while dozens of online news publications, from *The Huffington Post* to Qatar-based *Al Jazeera*, have been blocked for expressing views counter to those of the UAE state.

It is not only about policing the tone or content of the comment or article; the UAE deems the very act of reporting or researching itself as criminal. In August 2016, the cybercrime law was amended to criminalize the use of a 'fraudulent IP address' to 'commit a crime or prevent its discovery,[8] leading many to worry whether using a virtual private network (VPN) to circumvent censorship could result in jail time.

Joe Odell, the Press Officer at the International Campaign for Freedom in the UAE, writes in *OpenDemocracy*[9] that for a brief moment, around the Arab Spring, the internet provided a space within Emirati society where debate, criticism and ideas thrived. 'A political opposition had begun to emerge in the "sleepy Emirates", which was previously dubbed the Switzerland of the Middle East for its relative internal stability and seemingly mediatory foreign policy agenda.' The acceptance of internet-enabled technology came early to the UAE—Apple and Google have headquarters in Dubai. There was 91 per cent internet penetration in 2016 in the UAE, and the government promised that it would become the world's leading hub of technological innovation. These trends made the UAE seem tech savvy, open and utterly progressive.

However, the same internet and technology have become repressive weapons.[10] 'The UAE authorities aggressively pursue anyone who doesn't toe the party line, and cyberspace has become their chosen hunting ground for critics and dissidents,' said Joe Stork, deputy Middle East director at Human Rights Watch. A June 2016 report from Citizen Lab,[11] a research institute at the University of Toronto that focuses on internet security and human rights, identified a series of digital campaigns against UAE dissidents, dating back to 2012. The government tightly controls the telecommunications industry, and holds large stakes in the country's two service providers, Etisalat and Du. These close telecom ties enable restrictions on Voice-over-IP (VoIP), rampant censorship and pervasive surveillance.[12]

One of the UAE's everyday surveillance tools came to light through the deceptively simple attempt to hack an internationally renowned pro-democracy activist's iPhone. On August 10, Ahmed Mansoor received a text message: 'New secrets about torture of Emiratis in state prisons.' This message was repeated eleven times, and included a link. If Mansoor had clicked on the link, it would have activated a software that would have turned his phone into a powerful surveillance tool for an entity that Citizen Lab researchers believe is the Emirati government.

Pegasus, the software used against Mansoor, can mine contact lists and read emails. It can track its subject's movements and remotely turn on the phone's camera and microphone. The software can even record phone calls and intercept text messages, including those on encrypted apps such as Viber and WhatsApp.

Citizen Lab identified several pieces of information suggesting a connection between the operator and the UAE government. In addition, Pegasus paid the NGO Group, a shadowy Israeli surveillance vendor, one million US dollars to hack into Mansoor's phone! The activist is now infamous as the 'million-dollar dissident'.[13]

In 2016, a Dubai police official himself announced that authorities were monitoring users across forty-two social media platforms.[14] The same year, Abu Dhabi launched Falcon Eye, an Israeli-installed civil surveillance system. (The foul irony here is that an Arab country joined hands with its otherwise enemy, Jewish Israel, to watch its own residents.) With this system, officials can monitor every person 'from the moment they leave their doorstep to the moment they return to it'.[15]

The Emirati surveillance state moved into the spotlight on 1 February 2018, as the Abu Dhabi-based cybersecurity company DarkMatter stepped out of the shadows to speak to the international media.[16] Established in the UAE in 2015, DarkMatter is a commercially driven company. However, the Emirati government makes up 80 per cent of its contracts. According to its website, the company's aim is to 'protect governments and enterprises from the ever-evolving threat of cyber attack'.

The company's founder and CEO, Faisal al-Bannai, told the Associated Press that DarkMatter was independent, although he acknowledged the firm's 'strategic business ties' to the Emirati government. The company, which hires former CIA and National Security Agency analysts, added that it left 'the ethical decisions about privacy and surveillance in wielding its powerful technology' to its customers, which include the Dubai police. In an investigation by *The Intercept* in 2016,[17] sources with inside knowledge said that DarkMatter's 'aggressive' plans included hiring skilled techies to exploit hardware probes already installed across major cities to track, locate and hack any person at any time in the UAE. In 2017, DarkMatter more than doubled its revenue to cross US$400 million, mostly through UAE government contracts.

While broad surveillance that violates people's right to privacy is on the uptick the world over, the Emirati government goes one step further: it also controls access to the internet. WhatsApp's voice feature was blocked in the UAE shortly after it was introduced in March 2015. Viber has been banned since 2013. Apple agreed to sell its iPhone products to UAE-based mobile phone companies without the Facetime application pre-installed. Users in the UAE reported that Skype and Viber only work over Wi-Fi, and Apple's Facetime video-calling feature can only be used if the iPhone was purchased outside the country. Discord, a chatting app used by gamers, had its VoIP feature blocked in March 2016. Snapchat voice services were blocked in April 2016.[18] In December 2016, Emirati authorities blocked the encrypted messaging app, Signal. Any user, including visitors to the UAE, found with the Signal app on their smartphone is liable to face suspicion and detention.

The government's ban on the use of VPNs for 'criminal' purposes exposes users to jail time or fines of up to US$540,000 for trying to evade censorship and surveillance. Ordinary people are often arrested for seemingly innocuous activities, such as uploading a photo of a poorly parked car or live-streaming a fire in a skyscraper. Thanks to the sweeping nature of this control, self-censorship is inescapable on social media. Most news sites also generally refuse to cover controversial issues. For instance, in February 2018, an Egyptian migrant worker tried to jump off a bridge in Dubai, with over a hundred people watching. The police arrived to detain him after a few hours. The next day, none of the local newspapers carried any report of the incident.

The 2017 annual report of Freedom House, a US-based non-profit that has (since 1972) ranked countries on their track record of upholding freedom of expression, declared the UAE 'not free'.[19]

The chief reason cited was the passing of a privacy-violating and punitive cybercrime law, and the subsequent detention of people for their political speech on social media. Academic Nasser Bin Ghaith received a ten-year prison sentence for several tweets deemed to ridicule, criticize or defame the UAE. A journalist was also sentenced to three years for insulting state figures on Facebook.[20] Human rights defender and twenty-nine-year-old blogger Osama al-Najjar was detained for online advocacy in support of his father, Hossein al-Najjar, a political detainee. Every day, an unknown number of activists and dissenters are being watched, or worse, being detained in the UAE.

*

Given the oppressiveness of Emirati life, it is remarkable that migrants continue to move to the country, and live and work there for years. In 2017, the UAE was the most sought-after destination for Indians, with more than 150,000 emigration clearances given. Desperate poverty is an often-quoted reason, but there is also aspiration, like a breath held. The hope of prosperity in a single generation seems to create an extraordinary tenacity in migrant workers.

Amid the silence of those who suffer abuse there, it is a handful of activists who speak for them. Even with increasing surveillance and crackdown, such well-wishers continue to take grave risks to expose exploitation and argue for political reform. One of the social workers who went to Deira that evening and spent hours listening to the migrant workers was himself detained for two days by the Dubai police; they took his phone and laptop for the entire duration. While on a short visit to India, where he could use his phone without fear of being tapped, he calls. 'They asked me for the names of other activists, kept calling me a criminal, [saying] that I was trying to bring a bad name to the country that sustained so many poor people from across the world,' he says. 'By the end of two days, I felt like a criminal.' He was released with a warning, but has lived in fear since then, going nowhere except the mall to buy groceries. In case he was being watched, he did not want to risk exposing migrant workers seeking help or other colleagues. 'The wonderful UAE not only exploits its migrants, but look at the amount of effort it puts into hiding it,' he says.

The repressive surveillance tools, in that sense, are the UAE's fig leaf. The country's political will to build and use surveillance tools to scuttle activism and criticism far outstrips its attempts to reform its labour practices. It spends far more resources and police manpower to track an individual social worker's movements, clamp down on good Samaritans trying to raise money for injured migrant workers and detain researchers than on developing an equitable economy.

'Technology can control people for a while, but what I worry about more are the bright lights, penthouses and unimaginable luxuries—they influence people slowly, and they have bought people's silence,' says the harassed social worker. 'For things to change, more liberal people in the UAE need to get angry,' he says. As the UAE's all-pervasive surveillance deepens, its liberal mirage is likely to fade.

Notes

1. Ramona Ruiz, 'Drivers driven to long hours by targets', *The National*, 25 April 2015.
2. Personal interviews.
3. Rothna Begum, *'I Already Bought You': Abuse and Exploitation of Female Migrant Domestic Workers in the United Arab Emirates,* Human Rights Watch, 22 October 2014.
4. According to the legal department of the Ministry of Human Resources & Emiratisation, 'Retaining workers' passport also amounts to forcible work in violation of the International Labour Organization (ILO) Convention on the Abolition of Forced Labour, to which the UAE is a signatory.' In 2002, the Ministry of Interior also issued a decree stating 'it will be considered as an illegal action to detain the passport in UAE except by the governmental parties'.
5. In 2016, the General Directorate of Residency and Foreigners Affairs said there were about 12,000 immigrants who had overstayed their visa. In 2017, it doubled to 25,000.
6. Rejimon K, 'Number of Indians committing suicide in Gulf countries rose to 322 in 2017, reveals RTI reply', *Firstpost.com*, 18 July 2018.

7. Froilan Malit and G. Naufal, 'Asymmetric Information under the Kafala Sponsorship System: Impacts on Foreign Domestic Workers' Income and Employment Status in the GCC Countries', *International Migration* 54 (5), pp.76-90, October 2016.

8. 'Dh 500,000 fine if you use fraud IP in UAE,' Emirates 24/7, 22 July 2016, http://www.emirates247.com/news/emirates/dh500-000-fine-if-you-use-fraud-ip-in-uae-2016-07-22-1.636441

9. Joe Odell, 'How Communication Technology Became a Tool of Repression: The case of the UAE, *OpenDemocracy*, 14 November 2017.

10. 'UAE is ranked "Not Free" on Internet Freedom'. Freedom on the Net 2017, Freedom House, https://freedomhouse.org/report/freedom-net/2017/united-arab-emirates

11. Bill Marczak and John Scott-Railton, 'The Million Dollar Dissident', The Citizen Lab, University of Toronto, 24 August 2016.

12. 'UAE in crackdown on social media abuse,' *Arabian Business*, 10 March 2015, http://bit.ly/1FKCiuW

13. Bill Marczak and John Scott-Railton, 'The Million Dollar Dissident', The Citizen Lab, University of Toronto, 24 August 2016.

14. 'Emirates Operate Online Police to Monitor Users', *Cairo Portal*, 24 February 2016.

15. Rori Donaghy, 'Falcon Eye: The Israeli installed mass civil-surveillance system of Abu Dhabi', *Middle East Eye*, 15 July, 2015, https://www.middleeasteye.net/news/uae-israel-surveillance-2104952769

16. Jenna McLaughlin, 'How the UAE Is Recruiting Hackers to Create the Perfect Surveillance State', *The Intercept*, 24 October 2016, https://theintercept.com/2016/10/24/darkmatter-united-arab-emirates-spies-for-hire.

17. Ibid.

18. UAE country profile, Freedom on the Net 2017, Freedom House, https://freedomhouse.org/report/freedom-net/2017/united-arab-emirates

19. 'UAE is ranked "Not Free" on Internet Freedom'. Freedom on the Net 2017, Freedom House, https://freedomhouse.org/report/freedom-net/2017/united-arab-emirates

20. 'UAE: Jordonian Journalist Convicted: 3-year sentence for insulting "state symbols" on Facebook' Human Rights Watch, 17 March 2017, www.hrw.org/news/2017/03/17uae-jordonian-journalist-convicted

'He Held A Gun to My Neck':

Modern Slavery and Forced Labour in the GCC

REJIMON KUTTAPPAN

'I just asked to go back to India and for the salary due to me. He held a gun to my neck and said that I am not going anywhere. He threatened that I will be killed and thrown into the sea...'

These are the words of Joomaila Beevi, an Indian migrant from Kerala, who had migrated to Saudi Arabia in 2015 with the hope of earning a little money to take care of her family back home. But after two years of hardship in Saudi, Joomaila returned to India empty-handed. She was subjected to forced labour and abused physically and mentally during her time in Saudi Arabia.

Joomaila had migrated to the Gulf through an illegal agent in the hopes of clearing the loans she had taken to marry off her daughter. 'The loan was around 300,000 Indian rupees [US$4,800]. So, when an agent approached me through a friend, I thought of accepting the offer. I was offered 20,000 rupees [US$320] as salary. The agent said the working conditions will be good. But I was fooled.'

A direct flight from Kerala to Saudi takes only six hours. But it took 336 hours—fourteen days—for Joomaila to reach the house in Madinah that would be her home, workplace and prison.

She started her journey on January 9, 2015, by taking a train from Thiruvananthapuram to Pune, which reached on January 12. The next day, on January 13, her agents tried to send her out of the country from Pune Airport. But that did not work out because the agents did not have officials known to them at the airport counters.

Instead, she was taken to Chhatrapati Shivaji International Airport in Mumbai to board a flight to Dubai. As the agents couldn't manage to get immigration clearance for her immediately, she had to stay in a hotel in Mumbai for five days, before she was successfully smuggled out of the country.

She stayed for a day and a night in Dubai, then was moved to Sharjah, and then flown to Bahrain. Joomaila was taken on a tourist visa to the UAE, which is an irregular pathway often used by traffickers. From Bahrain, she was finally flown to Madinah, arriving fourteen days after leaving Thiruvananthapuram. 'I stayed in scary hotels and apartments, slept alone in airports and reached Madinah on 23 January night,' Joomaila said.

Migrant workers who arrive in the destination countries through such irregular routes are often subjected to contract duplication, travel document seizure, physical and mental abuse, non-payment of salary, unremitting toil and modern slavery. In Joomaila's case, she faced a constant barrage of abuse, was expected to work from morning to night without rest, despite falling ill for several months, and was denied her wages. One day, while the employer's family was out, she called a social worker whose number she had been given by another domestic worker and told him the whole story. He advised her about her options; the risks of running away, and the possibility of taking shelter in the Indian embassy.

'As it was quite difficult to continue there, I had to flee,' Joomaila recalled. She left the house, grabbing only her phone and an abaya to cover herself. Runaway domestic workers are often framed for theft by the employer in the GCC countries. 'I didn't take anything else. I knew that even if I take my own things, they will file a case of theft against me. I was not well. I had some swelling in my legs and irritation in my throat. It got worse as I was denied medical assistance. I was afraid of dying there. I just wanted to go back home. So, I didn't want to complicate things by landing in theft cases,' Joomaila said.

She had informed the social worker that she would try to reach the Indian embassy, and he had alerted them, so that they were ready for her. She stayed in the embassy shelter for a month, while they processed her repatriation papers, so that she could return to India. The social worker also helped to file an official complaint on her behalf with the Ministry of External Affairs in New Delhi, which further encouraged the Indian embassy in Saudi Arabia to help her.

After having worked for almost two years, Joomaila received only six months' salary. After her return to India, even though she wanted to file a case against the recruiters who trafficked and duped her, she had to agree to a meagre amount as compensation and drop the case, due to her financial situation. 'I have to look for a job. When the police call me to attend hearings, I may not even have money for transport to reach the station. So, I withdrew the case,' Joomaila explained.

The forty-eight-year-old widow now survives mainly on what her aged parents and siblings earn in their thatched-roof home in Kerala. She works as a midwife to earn a little money.

In mid-2018, Joomaila was diagnosed with throat cancer. 'If they had given me medical care at the proper time, my disease would not have worsened this much. I suffered a lot with throat pain for nine months in Saudi Arabia. They didn't care at all,' she lamented.

She lost her share of the family land in Kerala as her siblings had to sell it to clear her loans. 'One of my brothers too gave up his share. It is due to their benevolence that I have shelter and food. I need around 1,000 rupees every fifteen days for medicine alone,' she said.

Joomaila's case is not an isolated one. The GCC countries have long been criticized for their treatment of migrant domestic workers.

Burnt and Bruised in Kuwait

Balla Padma Pande, an Indian domestic worker from East Godavari district in Andhra Pradesh, returned empty-handed from Kuwait with burns and bruises after being enslaved for nearly seven years.

Padma had gone to Bahrain in 2003, Dubai in 2006 and later, to Kuwait in 2009, with high hopes. But luck was not on her side.

'Everything was okay for two years, till my employer was alive. After his death, the wife got married to another person. The new person was quite arrogant. He, my late employer's wife and her son started to abuse me physically and mentally,' Padma said. According to Padma, she was not given a phone to contact her family or her husband, who was working in Dubai as a painter. She was not allowed to step out of the house or talk to any neighbours. 'It was jail. Really a jail…' she recalled.

When queried as to why nobody from her family had approached the Indian authorities, she said that all of them were illiterate and might have thought that she had gone 'missing' or died. 'Only my aged in-laws are there at home. They might have been clueless about what to do,' she explained. Additionally, as her husband was on a work visa, he was unable to travel from Dubai to Kuwait to look for her.

After seven years of 'house arrest', on November 11, 2017, Padma found the hidden location of the door key and early in the morning of November 12, took the key discreetly, opened the door and ran away.

Unfortunately, as she was not well she could not walk for very long and fainted. 'I fell down unconscious on the road. Somebody informed the police, they took me to a hospital and I was admitted there for a week. They took a statement from me and moved me to the Indian embassy shelter. With the embassy officials and social workers' help, I am now on my way home,' she added.

Confirming her travails, a senior official at the Indian embassy in Kuwait said that she had undergone severe mental and physical torture. According to the official, who wished to remain anonymous, Padma had come to Kuwait in 2009 on a domestic worker visa. Sister Lissy Joseph of the National Workers' Welfare Trust in Hyderabad, who filed the grievance petition for Padma's repatriation, also confirmed that she had undergone unbearable torture.

Once she was safely at the embassy shelter, the embassy officials and the Kuwait Police both advocated on Padma's behalf. 'We took up the case with Kuwait's Manpower Ministry, too, with the involvement of the Kuwait Human Rights Society,' the official added.

Padma has given a power of attorney to claim her salary of 10,000 Kuwaiti dinars (around US$33,000) to a lawyer with the Kuwait Human Rights Society. She was earning around 10,000 Indian rupees per month (US$135), which she got only for the first two years (2009–2011). She claimed that she was not paid even a single penny after that.

Even though Kuwait is the first country in the GCC to have a labour law for domestic workers, activists claim that the law often fails to protect the workers' rights. According to a document submitted in the Indian Parliament in August 2017, there were 1,206 complaints registered by exploited Indian women in Kuwait.

'Kuwait has set US$200 as a minimum salary for migrant domestic workers, but many don't get the minimum wages in practice,' says Rafeek Ravuther, a migrant rights activist and director of the Kochi-based Centre for Indian Migrant Studies (CIMS). And with domestic workers at the mercy of their employers behind the closed doors of private homes, these regulations are difficult to monitor and implement.

Padma has also filed a criminal case for physical and mental abuse. The embassy official said that her sponsors, the two Kuwaitis who tortured her, have been jailed.

An Indian lawyer in Kuwait, who also requested anonymity, said that usually such cases take three to five years to reach a conclusion. 'Moreover, it all depends on how strongly the petitioner's lawyer can prove the abuse evidence in the court, which sometimes is quite hard. However, cases don't take much time, like in India. Maximum, it is five years,' he added.

'When we were informed by social workers in Kuwait about Padma, we started filing petitions officially to repatriate her. It started in November 2017 and now she is back home,' Sister Lissy said in February 2018. It is sobering to realize that despite the brutality and hardships she faced, Padma is one of the lucky ones, since she was able to escape. Many other men and women remain in conditions of bondage throughout the GCC.

Trafficking and Forced Labour

In 2017, Human Rights Watch[1] interviewed several women working in the GCC, who said that their employers confiscated their passports, withheld their salaries, forced them to work without rest times or days off, and subjected them to psychological, physical and sexual abuse. In some instances, the abuses amounted to forced labour or trafficking.

According to the International Labour Organisation's statistics,[2] women and girls are disproportionately affected by forced labour, accounting for 99 per cent of victims in the commercial sex industry and 58 per cent in other sectors.

According to migrant rights activists, hundreds of Indian women are still lured by recruiters, duped and trafficked to six GCC countries: Oman, Saudi Arabia, Kuwait, Bahrain, Qatar and the UAE. In some cases, Indian women are also trafficked to Lebanon and Jordan, where they are subjected to forced labour.

Ravuther said CIMS came across eighty-six cases of women who had gone missing after travelling to these countries in 2016. 'Out of the eighty-six cases, thirteen are still missing in the Gulf countries,' says Ravuther, who was involved in Joomaila's rescue. 'I filed official complaints with the Indian authorities and with their help, found the whereabouts of the [rest of the] trafficked women and brought them back with assistance from the Indian embassy officials and social workers in the host country.'

Ravuther said that the UAE is often used as an entry point for trafficking across the GCC, as entering there is easier, compared to entering via other countries. 'Women can be taken to the UAE easily on a tourist visa and then "sold" to employers in other countries,' he explained.

According to Ravuther, as trafficked women are brought to the Gulf through irregular channels, it is easier for them to go missing, and the chances of them being subjected to forced labour are higher as well. And even if they are subjected to forced labour, none of them will be able to prove it legally and claim compensation because, according to government records, they have not migrated at all.

In a bid to fight this, the Indian government has launched several campaigns to educate potential migrants, especially women domestic workers, on the need for safe migration. Several videos and official tweets advised Indians to migrate only through official recruitment agencies and to get in touch with the Indian embassy once they arrive in the foreign country.

The Indian government also attempted to put in place several steps to safeguard the interests of Indian women workers migrating to Emigration Clearance Required (ECR) countries, including Kuwait, in view of complaints about the exploitation and harassment of domestic sector workers by unscrupulous agents and employers. For example, in 2015, the Indian government initiated the eMigrate system, a safe and official recruitment channel for those who want to migrate abroad for a job, especially to the eighteen Arab and North African countries which have signed up to the ECR system.

Unfortunately, certain processes in the eMigrate system that were required to recruit women as domestic workers were removed. In September 2017, for instance, India removed the requirement for foreign employers to give a US$2,500 bank guarantee if they wanted to recruit Indian women as domestic workers, leaving women migrant workers in more trouble.

The bank guarantee norm had been implemented in 2014 as a welfare move. It had acted as a shield for women domestic workers if the employer failed to pay wages, or if the domestic worker was subjected to abuse and required compensation and financial aid to return home. However, employers in Kuwait were reluctant to follow the norm and the Kuwait government also banned the recruitment of Indian women domestic workers in 2015. As a result, India withdrew the rule.

According to the senior official in the Indian embassy in Kuwait, when this financial guarantee requirement was lifted, the Kuwait media reportedly misunderstood the decision and reported that the government's ban on Indian women domestic workers had also been lifted.

Some of the GCC governments have made efforts to improve the situation of domestic workers. In 2013, Saudi Arabia issued regulations entitling domestic workers to at least nine hours of rest during every twenty-four-hour period, with a weekly day off and paid vacation after two years, according to Human Rights Watch.[3] However, these attempts are not enough to guarantee their basic rights, according to rights groups. And the irregular pathways for trafficking women migrant workers continue to exist.

Contract Duplications

Men are also subjected to forced labour in ways that are hard to see and even harder to measure.

Sometimes, recruitment agents and sponsors trick the embassies of the countries where they find labour. For example, even though the Indian embassy in Kuwait has stopped allowing Indians to enter on shepherd visas, Indians are brought to Kuwait on domestic worker visas and then forced to work as shepherds, a particularly isolated job that leaves them at the mercy of their employers. An official at the Indian embassy in Kuwait City said, 'We have stopped issuing clearances for shepherd visas. But still, we come across cases of Indians working as shepherds and they are being abused physically and mentally.'

Rajayah Yenkampally, a forty-three-year-old native of Andhra Pradesh, migrated to Kuwait in 2016 on a domestic worker visa, but was forced to work as a shepherd in the Wafra desert on the Kuwait–Saudi border. Though not happy at the prospect of looking after over a hundred goats all by himself in the harsh desert, he had little choice but to continue with the work. Until, one day, a goat went missing and he was beaten up by his employer.

'Just one goat had gone missing...I informed the sponsor. He pushed me down and banged my head on the floor. I could taste my blood, my entire face was covered with it...I was losing consciousness too...' Yenkampally recalled.

Yenkampally's employer took him to the hospital, but when he realized that he would be held responsible for the assault, he abandoned Yenkampally and fled the scene.

As Yenkampally's identity documents were kept by his employer, the hospital denied him advanced care. 'Helpless, I left the hospital. Due to dizziness, I was not able to walk either. Luckily, an Indian driver approached me and took me to the Indian embassy. With their help, I was again taken to the hospital and provided proper treatment.' The Indian embassy then provided Yenkampally shelter.

Like Yenkampally, Mohammed Kasim, a twenty-five-year-old Kashmiri from the Poonch area, and Mohammed Bilal, a forty-year-old Bangladeshi, were brought to Kuwait by agents as domestic workers, but then thrown into the desert and forced to work as shepherds.

None of the shepherds I spoke to had his passport with him, and most were not confident that they could easily access it.

Confiscating Travel Documents

According to the ILO[4], forced or compulsory labour is any work or service that is exacted from any person under the menace or threat of a penalty, and which the person has not entered of his or her own free will. The ILO states that migrant workers being coerced to work through the withholding of their passports or identity documents can also be considered as forced labour.

The ILO also says that employers may hold the workers' identity documents for safekeeping; however, in such cases, the worker must always have access to the documents, and there should be no constraints on the ability of the worker to leave the enterprise.

Kuwait has ratified ILO's forced labour convention C29 and the abolition of forced labour convention C105, in 1968 and 1961, respectively.[5] According to Kuwait's ministerial decision 143/A/2010,[6] passports cannot be confiscated by the sponsor. Additionally, a domestic worker visa cannot be converted into a shepherd visa or a farm job visa.

In 2016, the United States classified Kuwait as a Tier 2 country in its annual Trafficking in Persons Report.[7] Kuwait had been classified as a Tier 3 country for nine consecutive years prior to this.

The latest report cites the passing of the 2015 domestic workers law and an unprecedented number of convictions of traffickers under the 2013 anti-trafficking law as reasons for the improved rating. But it also found that Kuwait's forced labour issues remain rampant and that victims of trafficking were still being arrested, detained and deported.

An RTI query filed in July 2017 has got a response from the Indian embassy in Kuwait, revealing that it received 2,287 complaints from Indian workers between January 1 to July 15 that year. 'Out of the total number of complaints received as indicated above, around 85 per cent were for non-receipt of salary and 95 per cent were about employers holding back passport of workers,' stated the reply.

*

Like the shepherds were left to the vagaries of the desert weather by their employers, around 5,000 Indians were left in the lurch by a construction company in 2016, forcing them to do menial jobs for survival. The migrant workers were stuck in Kuwait for over eighteen months without food, water or adequate shelter till an amnesty was announced on January 29, 2018, finally allowing them to leave the country.

'For the last eighteen months, embassy officials and ministers are coming and going. We hear the same words. We will be rescued soon, help is on the way, no need to worry… But now we are scared that we will die here without seeing our family,' said the Indian workers of the Kharafi National Company, which had partially shut down its operations at the end of 2015, citing economic hardship due to the global dip in oil prices. As a result, around 1,800 Indian workers, mainly from south Indian states, who had resigned from the company, were stranded without proper food, drinking water, accommodation, money and most importantly, travel documents. An additional 3,614 Indian workers, predominantly from the blue-collar sector, have filed complaints to get their unpaid salaries, after waiting in the vain hope of being paid for several months.

A senior official from the Indian Embassy in Kuwait said that as the amount pending in unpaid salaries was quite high, there was not much hope of the company paying up. 'We have calculated the pending salary for the workers as 8 million Kuwaiti dinars [approximately US$26 million]. We are trying our best to get it for the workers,' the embassy official said in October 2017. A few hundred workers got their dues later, in mid-2018, but most remain unpaid. Even if the workers get the salaries due to them, many of them have also to repay the loans that they took to survive in the interim.

Although the Indian Minister of External Affairs had visited Kuwait more than once to find a solution to the stranded workers' issues, no positive action or results transpired for over a year. Meanwhile, the stranded workers said that it was getting harder by the day for them to manage.

'I came here with great hope. Worked for more than eight years. Now, the company is not paying us for the last one year. They are saying that they don't have money. Top level management is missing, and the mid-level guys tell us that they are helpless,' complained Jose P., a worker from Kerala. He has a family to take care of and his son's engineering course had been in limbo due to non-payment of fees. Jose could not leave Kuwait either, because his passport was being held by the company.

Even if he had got it back from them, he would have had to pay around 80,000 Indian rupees (US$1,081) in fines for overstaying with an expired resident card. 'The overstaying issue came up when the company failed to renew our resident cards and the workers were left to suffer,' he claimed.

Shaheed Sayyed, an Indian social worker in Kuwait, said that some of the workers were not physically well, and others had emergencies back home that required their presence. But none of them had their passports. 'A few days ago, one worker's father passed away and today [January 15, 2017] another similar case has happened. In both cases, the workers couldn't go back,' she said.

Rajesh S., a migrant worker from Tamil Nadu, wanted to return immediately, no matter what the cost. 'I have severe stomach pain. I need advanced treatment. So, I have decided to go home. And the only way to make it happen is spend money from my own pocket to pay the overstaying fines and so get the passport to leave the country,' said Rajesh.

The workers employed by the Kharafi company have been subjected to forced labour as their passports are being held back restricting their freedom of movement, violating ILO norms. In fact, ministry resolution number 143/A/2010 clearly states in Article 1: 'It is prohibited for private sector employers and oil sector employers to hold travel documents of their employees.' But in Kuwait, which follows the kafala system—the bonded labour system—most workers must surrender their passports to their employers on arrival itself.

Kafala, the Bonded Labour System

The GCC countries provide visit visas depending on the nationality, job and financial status of the foreigner. While most GCC countries provide visas on arrival for US and EU citizens, citizens from Asian countries, including India, are not given that preferential treatment. Instead, they are usually subject to the kafala system, a 'sponsorship system' that ties the legal residency of workers to their employers.

The kafala system emerged in the 1950s to regulate the relationship between employers and migrant workers in many countries in West Asia. The sponsorship system's economic objective was to provide temporary, rotating labour that could be rapidly brought into the country in economic boom and expelled during less affluent periods. It remains a routine practice in the GCC and in the Arab states of Jordan and Lebanon.

Inherent in the kafala system is the assumption that workers are considered temporary contract labour. This is also reflected in the GCC's official use of terms such as 'guest workers' and 'expatriate manpower' to refer to migrant workers.

The kafala system thus serves a social purpose by institutionalizing the temporary nature of a migrant worker's presence, so that even if the worker has been in the country for a long time, she doesn't have avenues to acquire the rights of citizenship. The restrictive immigration policies of the kafala system act, in theory, to limit the stay of overseas workers in the country to the duration of their contract. However, non-compliance by both employers and migrant workers in response to the demand for labour has led to a significant minority of long-term or permanent residents, along with a significant number of second-generation migrants. It has also led to a flourishing underground economy based on irregular employment.

Under the kafala system, a migrant worker's immigration status is legally bound to an individual employer or sponsor (Kafeel) for their contract period. She or he must be sponsored by a Kafeel to enter the destination country and remains tied to this Kafeel throughout her or his stay. The migrant worker cannot enter the country, transfer employment nor leave the country for any reason without first obtaining explicit written permission from the Kafeel. This makes migrant workers completely dependent upon their Kafeel for their livelihood and residency.

Often, the Kafeels exert further control over the migrant workers by confiscating their passport and travel documents, despite legislation in some countries that declares this practice illegal. In addition, Kafeels must report to the immigration authorities if migrant workers leave their employment and must ensure that workers leave the country after the contract ends, including paying for the flight home.

The Kafeel's immense control and unchecked leverage over workers creates an environment ripe for human-rights violations and erosion of labour standards. If the migrant worker decides to leave the workplace without the employer's written consent they may be charged with 'absconding', which is a criminal offense. Even if a worker leaves in response to abuse, they remain at risk of being treated as a criminal rather than receiving appropriate victim support. In addition, they are unable to leave the country, since this would require possession of their passport and the employer's consent. Thus, migrant workers may remain for years in this vulnerable situation, living with the threat of unpaid wages, arrest, or detention and, ultimately, deportation, should they complain or leave.

The kafala system affects 23 million migrant workers across the Middle East, where many are trapped in slavery-like conditions when their wages are stopped, and they are unable to leave because employers have confiscated their paperwork.

ILO says that forced labour is any work or service that is exacted from any person under the menace or threat of a penalty, and which the person has not entered of his or her own free will. Deciding whether work is performed voluntarily often involves looking at external and indirect pressures, such as the withholding of workers' identity documents, including their passport. Thus, the power that the kafala system delegates to the sponsor over the migrant worker has been likened to a contemporary form of slavery.

Modern Slavery: A Snapshot

Although modern slavery is not defined in law, it is used as an umbrella term that focuses attention on the commonalities across these legal concepts. Essentially, it refers to situations of exploitation that a person cannot refuse or leave because of threats, violence, coercion, deception and/or abuse of power.

According to the ILO,[8] at any given time in 2016, an estimated 40.3 million people were in modern slavery, of which 24.9 million were subject to forced labour and 15.4 million in forced marriages. This means there are 5.4 victims of modern slavery for every 1,000 people in the world. One in four victims of modern slavery are children.

Of the 24.9 million people trapped in forced labour, 16 million are exploited by the private sector in areas such as domestic work, construction or agriculture; 4.8 million are subject to forced sexual exploitation; and 4 million in forced labour imposed by state authorities.

Among cases where the type of work was known, the largest share of adults in forced labour were domestic workers, almost a quarter of the total. This was followed by the construction (18 per cent), manufacturing (15 per cent), and agriculture and fishing (11 per cent) sectors.

Except for domestic work, the proportion of men in forced labour is greater than women in sectors involving manual labour.

One quarter of male victims of forced labour were in the construction sector (25 per cent), followed by 21 per cent in manufacturing, 16 per cent in domestic work and 13 per cent in agriculture and fishing.

Over one-third of female victims of forced labour were exploited for domestic work (36 per cent), followed by 21 per cent in hospitality and food services, and 11 per cent in the wholesale and retail trade sector.

Most victims of forced labour suffer multiple forms of coercion from employers or recruiters.

Nearly one quarter (24 per cent) had their wages withheld or were prevented from leaving by threats of non-payment of due wages.

Threats of violence are suffered by 17 per cent, acts of physical violence by 16 per cent, and threats against family are made in 12 per cent of the cases. Among women, 7 per cent of the victims reported acts of sexual violence.

The global trade in human beings is larger today than at any time in history. The United Nations says that modern slavery is an industry worth more than US$150 billion in illegal profits a year.

Notes

1. https://www.hrw.org/news/2017/06/16/gulf-states-slow-march-toward-domestic-workers-rights
2. www.ilo.org/global/topics/forced-labour/lang--en/index.htm
3. http://gulfmigration.org/decision-no-310-of-1434-on-domestic-workers/
4. https://www.ilo.org/global/topics/forced-labour/news/WCMS_237569/lang—en/index.htm

5. https://www.ilo.org/dyn/normlex/en/f?p=NORMLEXPUB:11200:
   0::NO::P11200_COUNTRY_ID:103423
6. http://indembkwt.org/Pages/images/Labour%20law.pdf
7. https://www.state.gov/documents/organization/258880.pdf
8. https://www.ailo.org/global/topics/forced-labour/lang--en/index.htm

Labour Migration from Bangladesh to Singapore

PORIMOL PALMA

Amidst the glitter of Singapore's high-rises, Saddam Hossain, a twenty-five-year-old Bangladeshi, sat on a concrete platform under a tree in the Little India neighbourhood. He looked sad and absent-minded.

'I don't have a job. I don't know if I will be sent back,' Saddam, a migrant worker, told me on a sunny morning in December 2017 as I sat with him. We had begun talking after I introduced myself as a fellow Bangladeshi. It was his second time in Singapore, but his job broker, also Bangladeshi, was dilly-dallying about placing him in a job. He had already been in the country for five days.

'I saw another Bangladeshi worker was sent back after cancelling his work permit. I am afraid I could be deported,' he said. The uncertainty about his future affected him badly, as he had to repay significant loans taken to finance his migration to Singapore. His brother-in-law had threatened to divorce Hossain's sister, when he could not repay the loan taken from them before his first attempt to migrate in 2014. His younger brother had to stop going to school and had begun working at a garment factory near Dhaka.

I took him to a nearby restaurant serving Bangladeshi food. There, Hossain detailed his history in Singapore since November 2014, when he first migrated there to work; the company's refusal to renew his work permit after a year; his return home, burdened with debt; and finally, his second migration to Singapore in December 2017.

From a Dream to Harsh Reality

After completing his secondary education in 2009, Saddam Hossain began working as an oven electrician and then a construction worker in his home city, Mymensingh, one of the larger cities of Bangladesh. His income gave him a bare livelihood but it was not enough to swiftly change the fortunes of his family, which depended on agriculture. While looking for better opportunities, he learnt through his friends of a training centre that promised Singapore-standard training and guaranteed highly-paid jobs in Singapore, which is widely perceived in Bangladesh as a well-governed country offering fair income for all.

In early 2012, an ambitious Saddam took admission in the training centre. Ideally, anyone wishing to go to Singapore needs no more than three months to complete the training, and can then take the skills test required by the Singaporean authorities. However, not all can sit for the test shortly after the training, because there are many more candidates than there is demand for labour in Singapore. Saddam was quick to learn the skills of aluminium formatting, but he had to wait for a year after the training to take the test.

He successfully passed the test. Then came the issue of recruitment in Singapore. Through an official at the centre, who was actually a broker working for a recruiting agent, he secured in-principle approval (IPA) for his work permit in Singapore. However, to get to this point, even before having a job offer in Singapore, Saddam had had to spend a total of 750,000 taka (US$9,375), including the training cost, which he raised by selling and leasing out land, selling trees and livestock, and taking loans to the tune of 300,000 taka (US$3,580). He showed me some photographs taken on his mobile phone before his first trip to Singapore. 'I just cry when I see these photos. What I was then, and what I am now,' Saddam sighed.

Nevertheless, he was happy to join ACL Group, a construction contractor, which supplied him to a piling company. The basic monthly wage for him was 429 Singaporean dollars (US$311). In practice, it totalled 650 Singaporean dollars (US$472), because he usually had to work two hours of overtime. The company provided a free dormitory, but he had to mandatorily pay 20 Singaporean dollars (US$14.50) for washing and 120 Singaporean dollars (US$87) monthly for food, regardless of whether he ate or not. 'The food quality was not good. So, I mostly bought food from outside,' he said, suggesting that his living costs simply went up. Thus, after taking into account expenses for food, a phone and other necessary items, he could send home 20,000 taka (US$250) a month. After four months, however, he was sent to two other companies, which increased his wages. On an average, he had to work three to four hours of overtime, so his monthly wage was close to 800 Singaporean dollars (US$581). He remained jobless for a month in between as well.

After Saddam had been in Singapore for a year, ACL denied the renewal of his work permit. 'I requested the company to provide me only the cost of food for the next year so that it renews my permit. I even pleaded for transferring my job to another company, but it said there was no system of transfer,' Saddam recalled.

The company sent him back to Bangladesh in November 2015. At the time, he was still indebted by more than 400,000 taka (US$4,773). With the family frustrated over his return in such circumstances, Saddam joined an unofficial training centre for Singapore-bound workers as a trainer. His monthly salary was 10,000 taka (US$125). That was too small an amount to recoup the loan. He kept trying to migrate to Singapore again, but only faced frustration. His contacts in Singapore kept him waiting for months. Finally, he managed another IPA for Singapore through a 'friend' (actually a job broker). This time, he spent 400,000 taka (US$4,773)—most of which went to brokers based in Singapore and Bangladesh.

However, a week after migrating to Singapore, he did not have a job, and the money he owed was increasing. 'How can I get rid of this danger?' he sobbed.

Southeast Asia as a Migrant Destination

An estimated 10 million Bangladeshis work abroad, mostly in the Middle East and Southeast Asia.[1] Bangladesh, a tiny South Asian country with 160 million people, which has maintained over 7 per cent GDP growth over the last several years, heavily depends on migrant remittances to maintain its balance of payments. While its macro-economy looks healthy, the well-being of its people, especially the marginalized ones, many of whom are migrants, remains questionable. The UN Human Development Index, which focuses on health and education and quality of life—as well as human rights perspectives—indicates that the experience of migrants in the GCC countries is not as positive as that in Southeast Asia, particularly Singapore. This essay draws on the experiences of migrant labour in Singapore and discusses the labour rights scenario there.

Recruitment Schemes

Saddam's is a classic example of the labour recruitment arrangement from Bangladesh to Singapore, which follows an ad-hoc, mostly unregulated pattern. It is riddled with corrupt practices and contributes to labour exploitation, forced labour and indebtedness. Though it is difficult to say what proportion of Bangladeshi workers going to Singapore actually achieve their dreams, one thing the migration experts say is that many of them are pushed into deeper poverty.

Costs of Recruitment

According to a survey on agent fees by Transient Workers Count Too[3] (TWC2), a Singapore-based charity, the average recruitment costs for Bangladeshi construction workers in first-time Singaporean jobs ranged from 5,500 to 11,000 Singaporean dollars (US$3,993–7,897) between 2007 and 2014. In 2015, this went up to a high of 15,555 Singaporean dollars (964,000 taka or US$12,055). In late 2015, TWC2 heard from Bangladeshi workers that the recruitment costs had become as high as 17,000 Singaporean dollars (1,020,000 taka or US$12,172), an unheard-of figure.

The survey, which was conducted in June and July 2016, says that only a few respondents could provide a breakdown of their total costs, but the general trend was that about half the amount would be used for skills training and the other half would go to 'agent fees'. The payments were almost all made in Bangladesh.

For subsequent jobs, the average recruitment fees each year ranged from 3,000 to 4,000 Singaporean dollars (US$2,178–2,904), between 2014 and 2016. The exception was in 2015, when the average was 4,299 Singaporean dollars (US$3,121). About half of the sixty-three respondents coming to take up subsequent jobs paid part or all of their costs in Singapore. Some said they had to pay their employers for their jobs.

Overall, migrant workers paid fees at several points: to training centres in Bangladesh; to agents and sub-agents in both Bangladesh and Singapore; and also, in many cases, to employers or their staff in Singapore.

Saddam Hossain had to spend 750,000 taka (12,500 Singaporean dollars or US$9,076) for his first migration to Singapore in 2014, which is in line with the survey findings. However, his recruitment expenditure during his second migration was 400,000 taka (6,666 Singaporean dollars or US$4,773), which is much higher than the average of 4,299 Singaporean dollars (US$3,121) reported by TWC2 for 2015. This indicates that the recruitment costs for subsequent jobs went up after 2015, as well.

Costs of Training

Singapore's Building Construction Authority (BCA) signed agreements with eight training centres in Bangladesh to provide training to Singapore standards in the late 1990s, as demand for trained workers was high in the construction and shipbuilding industries. The levy paid by companies hiring foreign workers was lowered for workers who had skills certificates. In July 2011, work permits for unskilled labourers in the construction industry were phased out, and in 2013, a two-tier levy rate was implemented across all sectors based on skills. In the construction industry, the levy for higher-skilled workers was 300 Singaporean dollars (US$218), as compared to 450 Singaporean dollars (US$327) for workers with basic skills. Employers, naturally, wanted to hire the more skilled workers.

With the rising demand for skilled workers, coupled with agents successfully enticing job-seekers with promises of lucrative salaries in Singapore, dozens of other training centres mushroomed around the BCA-approved ones. It didn't matter whether workers really needed the skills, or whether too many workers were being trained, compared to the actual demand for labour in Singapore. The Migrant Security Foundation (MISAF) Bangladesh, an NGO, found around 100 such training centres in the peripheries of Dhaka in 2013.[2] The survey showed that these unapproved training centres had about 500 trainees each, at any given time.

A young man* wishing to take admission to an approved training centre needs to fork out 50,000 to 100,000 taka (about US$597–1,193). In addition, he has to pay for incidentals, including books, uniforms, accommodation and meals. TWC2's interviews with Bangladeshi workers in Singapore indicate that they paid around 3,000 Singaporean dollars (US$2,178) for their courses, excluding incidentals. Hassan Ahamed Chowdhury Kiron, secretary general of Singapore Manpower Agencies Association, admitted there are training centres beyond the eight approved by the BCA of Singapore. He said the formal charges for training a candidate are 120,000 taka (US$1,500). But the unapproved training centres charge 400,000 to 500,000 taka (US$4,773–5,967).

MISAF found that unofficial training centres send their students to an authorized test centre to take the tests they need to be eligible to migrate to Singapore. However, some workers reported that BCA's testers came to their unofficial training centres to conduct tests. This means that the BCA is fully aware of the presence of dozens of unofficial training centres.

At most, 1,000 candidates can sit for the tests each month, but the training centres prepare forty to fifty times that number of aspirants. MISAF's survey finds indications that the training centres in effect auction the test slots to their trainees. Those who are prepared to

---

*Only male workers undertake such skills training to go to Singapore from Bangladesh.

pay more get earlier dates for tests, while others can remain in the waiting list for as long as a year and a half. Saddam Hossain phrased it this way: 'Training centres talk of buying a quota [of seats] from Singapore. So, we have to pay more.'

Costs of Job Brokers

Once aspiring migrants pass the test, they need to find jobs. For Singapore, again, they are dependent on the training centres, which require aspirants to deposit their passports with the centre. According to Saddam and other migrant workers, these training centres act like recruiting agents. In other words, the training centres or certain officials there are either officially or unofficially linked to the other brokers and recruiting agents that process job documents for Singapore-bound workers. TWC2 says that the control over the passport effectively eliminates the possibility of the worker finding another recruiting agent. In this way, the training centres monopolize the recruitment of workers to Singapore. Only fourteen of the more than 1,000 licensed recruiting agents in Bangladesh recruit workers for Singapore.

Kiron said that some Singaporeans, in connivance with Bangladeshis, open companies in Singapore that exist in name only. Such companies sometimes hire workers from Bangladesh, deploying brokers who basically trade in work visas. That explains why job visas for Singapore have become very expensive.

Singapore's Ministry of Manpower (MoM) responded to questions about this practice in an email, saying that it has laws prohibiting middlemen in Singapore, or any persons, including employers and employment agencies, from demanding or receiving monies or other benefits from foreign workers as a condition of employment. In 2012, Singapore raised the penalty for the collection of kickbacks from a fine of up to 5,000 Singaporean dollars (US$3,630) or imprisonment for up to six months, or both, to a fine of up to 30,000 Singaporean dollars (US$21,782) or imprisonment for up to two years, or both. To further protect migrant workers, the law presumes that any monies collected from migrant workers are collected as consideration of employment, unless the employer or employment agency can prove otherwise. The MoM's response mentioned that, in October 2017, a company director was sentenced to six weeks' imprisonment for collecting kickbacks from six migrant workers as a condition for their continued employment with the company. In the past five years, about forty employment agencies have been prosecuted or fined, or issued with warnings for over-charging migrant workers. With such measures in place, cases of over-charging have halved over the last three years, said the MoM in December 2017.

While the MoM reports Singapore's strict laws against this practice, it also admitted that it has been prosecuting agents for over-charging migrant workers, indicating that, as reported by various migrants, the practice is very much present.

Job Conditions in Singapore

Until 2005, the recruitment of migrants from Bangladesh was below 10,000 per year, except in 1997, 1998 and 2000. When the global economic downturn of 2008 was causing havoc on jobs across the world, including in Singapore, the number of Bangladeshi workers going to this Southeast Asian country rose.

Migration from Bangladesh to Singapore

Year	Number of Bangladeshi migrants to Singapore
2006	20,139
2007	38,324
2008	56,581
2009	39,581
2010	39,053
2011	48,667
2012	58657
2013	60,057
2014	54,750

Year	Number of Bangladeshi migrants to Singapore
2015	55,523
2016	54,305
2017	40,401

Source: Bureau of Manpower Employment and Training (BMET)

Overall, between 1979 and 2017, over 700,000 Bangladeshis migrated to Singapore. At the end of 2017, the number of Bangladeshis in Singapore was between 120,000 and 160,000. This indicates that some 550,000 workers returned from Singapore. Of course, many of them migrated to Singapore a second and even a third time. However, the most crucial questions are:

a) How and why were such a high number of workers recruited by Singaporean employers? And, following from this,

b) How did the Singaporean authorities approve such a high rate of worker recruitment during the financial crisis, when the demand for labour fell?

Oversupply of Migrant Workers

Kiron's description of the spurious in-name-only companies is relevant here. These companies that survive mostly on recruiting migrant workers, especially Bangladeshis, make a significant contribution to the oversupply of workers to Singapore. 'Once [the migrant workers] land in Singapore to work in such companies, they don't find jobs. Or, they are sent to other companies or kept in godowns [confined dormitories]. After one or two months, they return or are forced to return,' said Kiron on May 11, 2018.

Bangladeshi workers and activists interviewed in Singapore in 2017 alleged that some Singaporean employers, along with their brokers and agents, make huge money out of such unscrupulous recruitment. The employers and agents are not actually interested in placing migrant workers in decent jobs, but only in making money out of their desire to migrate. For them, it does not matter whether the workers get fair wages, or if the employers renew their visas. Since Singapore allows employers to terminate the contracts of migrant workers at will, they can simply cancel the visas.

The MoM said that, due to economic restructuring and low oil prices, the construction and marine sectors in Singapore have experienced high rates of retrenchment, affecting local and foreign workers alike. The response suggests that for the businesses to be competitive, any retrenchment is rational. But it is clear that no-one is looking out for the protection of migrant workers.

In an interview, Debbie Fordyce, executive committee member of TWC2, who has been involved with the charity since 2006, said:

> When I first started a food programme in 2008, I saw Bangladeshis in their hundreds coming, paying for jobs that provided them with no work and, of course, no salary. Singapore's way of dealing with that was to simply send them home. It was 2008–2009. The numbers started to reduce in 2010.
>
> It seemed clear that the companies had no intention of giving them work. When they came to us, they said there was no work and no pay. In those days, they paid 5,000 to 8,000 [Singaporean] dollars [US$3,630–5,808] to come here for a job. And they were sent back after one or two months. Some of them said that the companies were to set up some sort of training programme. But it seemed like a delaying tactic.
>
> I think that the Singapore government didn't know how to deal with that. The men were sent home, though they had six to seven family members depending on them. Some of the companies were taken to task, but many of them would close down and set up again with a different name. It's not as bad as that now.
>
> We do still see some companies that are not able to provide work for the men after they come. There are various things that the men can do. They can find their own work illegally, and suffer the consequences. We still see non-payment and underpayment of salaries, and demands for kickbacks, demands for money for work-permit renewals. We see [...] those who come with workplace injuries. It might be that the men who were injured had decided to make do with the low salaries until they were injured. When

they were no longer able to work because of the injury, then they decided to raise the issue of salary as well.

Asked if there is a syndicate that brings the workers to Singapore just to make money, she said:

> That's the way I see it. It seems to be how it works. It's not as bad as it was ten years ago. In those days, it happened at a much larger scale. Nowadays, it does appear that the MoM will take issue with companies who terminate their workers before six months. So, we see some workers are being terminated in the seventh month. But, we don't see such terminations on such a large scale.
>
> We do still see workers who suffer from lower salaries than they were promised and a certain number of them coming on IPAs and not receiving jobs. The MoM is looking into it a little bit more carefully now. It now provides [migrant workers] a chance to find another employer if the worker is already here. But the problem with that approach is that nobody wants to give you a job for free. Most of the men we know who have been given a chance to transfer jobs say that they are asked to pay 2,000 to 4,000 [Singaporean] dollars [US$1,452–2,904] to the new employer. If that employer had employed a new man from Bangladesh, they would have been paid that amount or more.
>
> Furthermore, employers don't want to take someone who has made a complaint to the MoM in the past, because he would be troublesome and ask for everything that he has a right to. Some employers say they don't want to take anyone who has been given the option of transfer by the MoM because they see him as a potential trouble-maker.

Low Wages and Wage Theft

Singapore has no minimum wage. The average basic monthly wage ranges between 300 and 600 Singaporean dollars (US$218–436) for migrant workers, as compared to between 4,493 and 5,808 Singaporean dollars (US$3,262–4,215) for citizens.

The MoM said that the government does not determine the wages received by workers, whether local or foreign. Wages are determined by the market and negotiated between employer and worker, depending on the workers' qualifications, skills and experience. It also said that migrant workers receive an IPA letter before they depart from their home countries for Singapore, informing them of their employment terms and conditions, so that they can make an informed decision on whether to take up the offer of employment. According to migrants, the agents usually don't provide the job contract to workers until just a day before they leave for Singapore, or even until they are at the airport to fly out. Such a fait accompli, coupled with the fact that not all migrants can read and understand the English used in the job contract, negates the point of issuing the IPA letter. Employers are not allowed to pay a lower salary than that stated in the letter, except with the worker's prior written agreement, but this is not enforced very strongly, according to Fordyce.

Fordyce says: 'Certainly among the foreign workers in Singapore, Bangladeshis pay higher amounts in cost to recruiting agents and receive the lowest salaries. We have seen salaries stated on application forms...they go to below 200 [Singaporean] dollars [US$145] a month...'

From migrant accounts and studies, it is clear that workers from Bangladesh pay very high recruitment fees and get the lowest wages in Singapore. Given this combination, Bangladeshi migrants require from twenty-six to fifty-one months to recoup the money they spent, according to a study by TWC2. Migrants therefore try their best to earn more by working overtime. However, that option is not always available. And even when it is, there is always a possibility of wage theft by the employers.

A study by Humanitarian Organization for Migration Economics (HOME) in 2017[3] found that many workers who go to HOME for assistance experience:

> multiple forms of wage theft and wage exploitation: unpaid wages for some months, short payment at other times, and unauthorized deductions throughout their employment. They may also be asked for kickbacks and are often not provided itemized pay slips, a copy of their employment contract (if there is one) or a full set of time

cards. When migrant workers finally decide to file a formal claim, they may have to contend with the surfacing of different forms of documentation that may be incomplete, fraudulent or contradict each other. Mediation processes, meanwhile, suffer from a lack of consistency and transparency, and often, a swift settlement is prioritized. Claims that proceed to Labour Court, meanwhile, present another set of problems, including the inability for workers to enforce judgment orders, even if they win their case.

Physical and Psychological Distress

Jolovan Wham, executive director of HOME, said that when a migrant worker gets low wages, he simply has to make do, regardless.

> He cannot eat adequate nutritious food. He cannot buy mutton or beef. He just has to eat less, and often food that's not of good quality. That's what you see when the workers come here. You compare the passport photos with how they look after they work here for a couple of months. You see such a big difference—a lot skinnier, much more tired, their skins have become a different colour. It affects their physical and mental wellbeing.

Often, migrants think they cannot afford to see a doctor or buy prescription drugs because of healthcare costs.

Eight out of ten migrant workers at higher risk of psychological distress in Singapore are from Bangladesh, says a study by the British medical journal, *Global Health,* published in 2017.[4] The study on 433 non-domestic migrant workers from Bangladesh, India and China conducted at clinics and a dormitory from July to August in 2016 shows that Bangladeshis form the vast majority of the 22 per cent of migrant workers under stress. In contrast, one out of ten from China and India says that he is under similar stress.

Forced Labour

The ILO has identified eleven indicators of forced labour: abuse of vulnerability; deception; restriction of movement; isolation; retention of identity documents; physical and sexual violence; withholding of wages; intimidation and threats; debt bondage;

abusive living and working conditions and excessive overtime.[5] Bangladeshi workers in Singapore are susceptible to most of these indicators, found a joint shadow report to the UN Committee on Migrant Workers by TWC2 and HOME, in 2017.[6]

The main cause of vulnerability to forced labour for these migrant workers is debt. They tend to work twelve to sixteen hours a day, if they find it possible, to reduce debt. Such indebtedness enables employers to use coercive power over workers, who are in a weak position to resist the employer's demands and exploitative practices. For example, there are many instances of migrant workers having to work excessive amounts of overtime to meet project deadlines. These conditions resemble debt bondage.

Complaints of intimidation and threats by employers—blacklisting, dismissal and deportation—are prevalent, states the report. Employers are also known to hire repatriation companies to confine workers and/or send workers home. Sometimes employers may also forcibly confine workers against their will.

Result: Pushed into Poverty

A.K.M. Mohsin, editor of the Bangla news magazine *Banglar Kantha*, says: 'Migrants are like candles. They burn themselves to provide light to others.' However, given the high recruitment costs and low wages, coupled with the prevalence of wage theft, one can see that most of the Bangladeshi migrants returning from Singapore might be being pushed into deeper poverty. I talked to over a dozen Bangladeshi migrants during my visit there in December 2017 and after returning to Dhaka. Most of them said that they had debts to be paid off still. They were concerned that the number of jobs in Singapore were shrinking and afraid that they might lose their jobs at any time and be sent home.

While there is no systemic research available on this topic, a study titled, 'In Quest of Golden Deer: Bangladeshi Transient Migrants Overseas' by Md. Mizanur Rahman, published in 2009, sketches a sad picture. It studies the financial benefits to migrants' families in Gurail, a village in southeast Dhaka, and finds that 80 per cent of returnee's families did not recoup the investment they made to send the family member abroad.

The Role of the Government

It is clear that modern slavery is alive in Singapore, despite its status as one of the world's most competitive business nations, enjoying modern development and high-end technologies. Singapore passes the blame for the situation onto the Bangladeshi authorities, for their failure to reduce the high costs of recruitment that are the root cause of many of the problems faced by Bangladeshi migrant workers. That blame is not entirely misplaced. HOME and TWC2 point out that Bangladesh's government has made no significant attempt to restrict the recruitment costs levied within Bangladesh, nor to intervene with the Singaporean authorities to stop the abusive practices and improve conditions in Singapore.

At the same time, there are a number of structural factors within Singapore that contribute to the poor socio-economic status of migrant workers. They include the presence of brokers and agents in Singapore. The lack of a minimum wage policy is also a big factor in determining the low salaries available to migrants. Those who lodge complaints with the MoM about salary deductions, non-payments and wage theft find it extremely difficult to prove the offences, as employers use variety of tactics to obfuscate the issue. While employers can terminate any migrant worker after six months, the workers have practically no other choice than to return, as changing jobs is equally not something that they can successfully negotiate. All these factors, which can be tackled by the Singaporean government if it desires, contribute to the vulnerability faced by migrants.

Neither Bangladesh nor Singapore has done anything significant to promote the well-being of migrant workers. Fordyce of TWC2 sums up the situation simply: 'Bangladesh is addicted to remittance and Singapore is addicted to cheap labour'.

Conclusion: An Open Question

Today, the age of globalization extols the virtues of privatization, deregulation, the free flow of capital, business competitiveness and technology. The government's role here is seen as a manager and regulator. When it comes to business and profit, this role is very small, but it is still acceptable as long as businesses trade in commodities. The problem emerges when labour—human beings with rights and human dignity—are traded.

In the case of labour recruitment from Bangladesh to Singapore, it is clear that a strong syndicate is engaged in trading people, the most important element of production. If privatization means trading in people, the question remains whether it is helpful to the advancement of civilization to embrace the slavery that the world has tried to abandon, centuries ago.

Notes

1. Bureau of Manpower Employment and Training.
2. http://twc2.org.sg/2013/09/22/training-centres-in-bangladesh-have-become-money-minting-machines/
3. https://www.csr-asia.com/newsletter-wage-challenges-faced-by-migrant-workers-in-singapore
4. https://www.ncbi.nlm.nih.gov/pmc/articles/PMC5435267/
5. https://www.ilo.org/global/topics/forced-labour/publications/WCMS_203832/lang--en/index.htm
6. http://twc2.org.sg/2017/10/03/home-and-twc2-submit-joint-report-on-the-exploitation-of-migrant-domestic-workers/

POLICIES

The Lottery of Migration

UPASANA KHADKA

Aspiring and current overseas Nepalese workers have a very high appetite for risk, given the higher-paying job opportunities abroad and the lack of alternatives domestically. In a maturing migration system like Nepal's, individuals are often aware of the common risks of migration, owing to social networks of current or former migrants, news and social media coverage of migration issues and migration awareness programs run by government and non-governmental organizations. However, many continue to make risky decisions, not always because of lack of information, but despite it. Mahesh,* a seasoned diaspora leader in Qatar who has watched migrants flourish and has himself rescued many from inhumane conditions that resemble modern-day slavery, attributes this to the culturally fatalistic view that migration is a lottery.

Indeed, this view of migration as a lottery echoed throughout my encounters with Nepalis at all stages of migration, whether aspirants, current migrants or returnees. Communities that had been struggling economically have transformed rapidly due to remittances, and this demonstration effect has influenced those left behind to consider migration as their ladder out of poverty. But the same communities are also full of stories of failed migrants duped by intermediaries, distressed migrants trapped in unfavourable terms of employment at the destination country and widows whose husbands returned in one of the four coffins that arrive daily from the GCC

---

*Last name redacted at his request

and Malaysia. Migration outcomes are consequently viewed as arbitrary and uncorrelated to individual decisions.

Economists like Michael Clemens and Lant Pritchett discuss migration in the context of the 'lottery of a birthplace' dictating economic opportunities handed to individuals and the concept of place premium i.e., the wage differential between two identical workers across borders.[1] Migration can be an equalizer of opportunity for those seeking better opportunities than what their birthplace affords, the driving factor for the 1,500 Nepalis leaving the country every day. But in addition to the lottery of a birthplace, the current migration governance system is mired in shortcomings and uncertainties such that those who were dealt an unfavourable hand and who attempt to migrate in search of better opportunities are faced with a second lottery: the lottery of migration.

Foreseeing the outcomes of migration can be a challenge. For many individuals, migration is not the predictable way out of poverty that it is supposed to be. The same intermediary who facilitates the migration process might place one client in a good job while failing another client. A worker may easily be able to repay the money borrowed to cover the upfront costs paid to a recruiter, while others with similar qualifications and job promises may struggle to repay it due to unpaid wages or lack of overtime hours. Some undocumented workers are able to live in the shadows for decades without getting caught and deported, whereas others are stuck in jails and detention centres. But what factors create the difference between these outcomes? There is much uncertainty about what gives one favourable odds of 'winning the lottery'—where a win comprises getting a job with the originally agreed employment terms being adhered to, and a loss can mean being trapped in some of the most vulnerable situations imaginable. And when it is not easy to predict these outcomes and attribute them to steps taken to get there, ideas like 'chance', 'fate' and 'luck' take centre-stage.

Sharmila, from Chitwan, a district with high migration rates, agreed with her agent to travel to Kuwait via India, to work as a maid. Given the Government of Nepal's blanket ban on migration for domestic workers, except to countries that have signed bilateral agreements with it, owing to safety and security considerations, she was convinced that this was her only way out. 'How else would I travel?' asked Sharmila, who knew very well that her journey entailed many risk points where she could potentially be caught by officials: at the India-Nepal border, at the Indian airport and at immigration control in the destination country. Stories of women getting stranded at these different points when taking the perilous journey are common in her community. If that concern was not enough to melt her resolve, her agent ensured that she was well-versed on the risks of taking this unauthorized channel. She briefed Sharmila on the do's and don'ts of crossing borders to minimize the chances of catching the attention of the border officials. *'Take only a small handbag with your passport and at the maximum, one spare pair of clothes so you don't raise suspicion—we will buy you clothes in Delhi once the coast is clear', 'Don't make eye contact with anyone and do not walk with other ladies you meet in the bus as that will draw attention', 'Walk briskly and try to be as invisible as possible'* and, in case of border control apprehensions, *'Say you are visiting family for a few days'.* The agent ensured that Sharmila understood that she would be putting both of them at risk if she raised suspicion among officials. These 'tips', instead of discouraging her, made Sharmila more inquisitive as she keenly tried to imbibe all the precautions that would ensure her safety. She was comfortable trusting this agent who was from the same community as her, but she was aware that the minute she crossed the border, she would have to entrust her life to strangers in the chain of agents scattered across the region. In desperation, migrants like Sharmila view even such unknown agents as their only ray of hope for a better chance at life in a faraway place, despite the stories of swindling, rape or disappearance that are rife.

For Sharmila, the courage to do the forbidden was fuelled by the possibility of what lay ahead at the destination country. If only she could cross the border, and somehow make it to Kuwait, she would be able to provide for her children—this was her last resort as her husband had abandoned her. 'My trip, which was supposed to take two days, took twenty-four days, spanning multiple countries including Nepal, India, Sri Lanka, the UAE and finally, Kuwait,' she recalled. 'In each country, we stayed in crammed rooms rented by the agent. We waited in vain every day for our names to be called out.' She painfully described how the agents would pick names randomly for a subset of women to continue on to the next leg of the journey.

'It was a relief to finally reach Kuwait, but even there, the agent's office was crammed with many women from across South Asia. We had to again wait to be picked by potential employers.' The employer who picked her ended up being exploitative, making her work from 4 a.m. to past midnight. She had no option but to escape, which she did with the help of a South Asian taxi driver. She returned to Nepal prematurely, distraught and without any savings.

When Ramesh from Okhaldhunga agreed to go on a visit visa—meant for tourists—to the UAE, he knew he was taking a chance. He also had to pay an inconceivable amount—US$2,500—to his agent for the gamble. It was apparent to him that he was being overcharged, especially since he had heard about the Nepal government's 'Free Visa, Free Ticket' policy that allows recruiters to only charge US$100 as service fees. US$2,500 was a huge amount to pay, especially since he raised the money by taking an informal high-interest loan at 36 per cent, but the larger than life possibilities that awaited at the destination country made it easy for Ramesh to convince himself and his family that the risks were worth taking. Furthermore, he knew he wasn't fit for the job that he'd been offered—he knew how to swim but wasn't a professional lifeguard, as required—but how could he let go of something that had already come to his hand in anticipation of an as-yet-nonexistent job that might be more suitable? He chose to take his chances and figure it all out when he reached the destination country. What was the worst that could happen, after all? The desire for the foreign land is so strong that it makes one myopic.

However, not only did his Dubai-based agent fail to find him a job, but he was verbally and physically abusive towards Ramesh. His only memories of Dubai now are the eighty-plus days he spent inside a cramped apartment—not wanting to overstay his visa, which had a validity of ninety days, he returned right before its expiration. Till date, he vividly recalls the sinking feeling in his stomach when he first saw the large number of flip-flops outside the apartment where he would be staying in Dubai. There were twenty-two other workers crammed into a small room for months. 'Space was so tight that you would have to worry about losing your spot to sleep if you went to the bathroom or for a walk,' he recalls.

Shama is twenty-four and looks sixteen. She holds a passport with a falsified age of thirty-two and when asked whether she knew this was wrong and could get her into trouble, she covers her face and laughs. Growing up in the mountainous region of Ghandruk, en route to the Annapurna range, she dreamt of escaping. The majestic view did not compensate for her gruelling job of carpet making, especially as she was aware that her employer was making a handsome amount while her daily wages were barely enough to cover the bare expenses of life. 'I had never left my village prior to that. The first time I went to Kathmandu was with the agent to make my passport,' she recalls. She knew she needed to get out of the village that often made her feel trapped, even if it meant trading the morning breeze for the heat of the Gulf. However, after flying out of Delhi due to the ban on domestic workers in Nepal, she couldn't make it past immigration in Dubai as it was easy for the officials to identify that there was something fishy about her presenting as a 'tourist' when she was unable to answer simple questions without getting perplexed. She was sent back to Kathmandu via Tribhuvan Airport, the very airport which she had initially avoided by travelling through India. 'I will again try after a few months,' she shares, convinced that just because she was unlucky once, it did not mean she won't succeed the next time.

The risk-taking does not end with leaving home. Nepali workers are taking risks even at the destination country. Ram's job in Malaysia

had no overtime provision, so, to earn more money, he switched
to an undocumented status which would expose him to distressing
circumstances—knowing fully well he would be deported if caught.
This is despite knowing how strictly the Malaysian government
had begun to crack down on unauthorized migrants, with periodic
raids at migrant hotspots that fuel a state of constant fear. Even in
that environment of high frequency raids and migrants getting
caught right and left, there is a belief among many undocumented
migrants, including Ram, that this won't happen to them. Otherwise,
many would opt for the exit pass that allows migrants without
documentation to leave the country. Ram was caught, spent six
months in detention and was sent back. He was among a group
of other deported Nepalis at Kathmandu airport, all empty-
handed, clad in t-shirts and flip-flops, walking with other Nepalis
pushing baggage carts with heavy suitcases and TV monitors. The
situation of these jailed deportees reveals the nature of this lottery
of migration—a first bad hand i.e., landing an abusive employer
or facing contract substitution, can be the start of many more bad
situations. The odds of winning keep getting slimmer as migrants
are relegated to the underground economy that entices them with
better prospects, but they end up digging themselves into a deeper
financial and security hole.

What makes these four Nepalis take risks are the lives of other
Nepali workers, who take the same steps or use the same agents
but are not caught. Shama talked to two women sent to Kuwait by
her agent who had landed good employers and encouraged her to
take the same route. Unlike Ram in Malaysia, Kul, who switched
to being undocumented, earned US$300 a month as a security
guard, double what he earned in his legal job at a furniture shop.
Further, he succeeded in dodging the immigration officials and
made it back safely to Nepal with a temporary out-pass. During
amnesties provided by governments of the destination countries,
a flood of Nepalis are seen to arrive in Nepal—they are the lucky
ones who did not get caught by the authorities for not having proper

documents. It is this possibility of being lucky that encourages so many to take risks.

*

Many migration policies fail to respond to migrants' aspirations and the ground realities which make foreign employment more like a lottery than a predictable pathway out of poverty. They fail to fully appreciate the high loans migrants take to arrive at the destination; how bound they are by the 36 per cent interest rate; how restricted their mobility is, especially under the Kafala system; or how desperate they are to make ends meet. They also fail to realize that no amount of discouraging information can prevent the migrants from taking a leap of faith, because migration offers the prospect of a bright future, a welcome alternative to the status quo. The process can be mentally taxing but as long as there is even a weak possibility of a better life for them and their families, their appetite for risk remains high. Major policies that were instituted with good intentions have instead had unintended consequences.

A case in point is the blanket ban on female domestic workers leaving Nepal, a contentious issue in Nepal's migration governance. Domestic work is viewed as a lucrative employment opportunity for many Nepali women. However, the Government of Nepal has often imposed bans on domestic workers since 2008. A look at these bans shows that they are usually implemented following isolated, high-profile stories of abuse faced by individual Nepali domestic workers. The ban, therefore, is well-intentioned and aimed at protecting its citizens because, in a scenario where the workplaces of housemaids are isolated and scattered, other interventions seem weak. However, the reality is that Nepal has an open border with India and no matter how strict a ban is imposed by Nepal, women will still find a way to leave via India. As a unilateral decision made with no coordination with the destination country, it is simply not effective. Nepali women leave Nepal unauthorized, but by the time they land in the destination country, they are legal and have all the required documents. This only puts our workers at risk because they are not registered in Nepal or at the embassy in the destination country nor are they covered by the protection measures that exist in Nepal's migration system for those who leave with legal permits.

Outlawing migration by domestic workers has driven recruitment underground, increasing the exploitation and risk for Nepali women. Domestic workers are already greatly vulnerable, given the isolated nature of their workplaces within the confines of homes. Many end up being trafficked en route, and spend days at the offices of agents whose business becomes more lucrative the tighter the ban. These agents' offices often become distribution points for trafficking workers to countries like Syria and Iraq, often unbeknownst to both the Nepalese government and the migrants and their families. Renu recalls her ordeal: 'At the agent's office in Kuwait, we were treated like goats. Employers walked in and checked us out, haggled and handed cash to the agent on the spot. We were sold like livestock.' The women are treated rudely by the agent if potential employers do not choose them. Women who are sent back by unsatisfied employers are treated even worse. 'My employer paid US$2,000 to my agent when she dropped me off at the employer's house, a day after she had picked me,' recalls Laxmi. Her employer called her a 'buffalo', physically abused her and did not pay her salary. She kept reminding Laxmi she had been purchased. In no way does the ban help in addressing such concerns because the tighter the ban, the more lucrative such underground markets, and the greater the uncertainty for migrant workers who take unauthorized channels and test their luck.

Not only has the ban affected new workers, it has adversely impacted current domestic workers abroad as well, including those who have perfectly good employers. Rita, a mother of three, recently lost her eighteen-year-old eldest daughter in Butwal. Her employers offered to buy her a ticket home for the funeral. But she could not leave Dubai, fearing she would not be allowed to fly back. 'I have a huge loan to repay, and as a single mother, still have to take care of my two other children, so how can I risk my job?' she sobbed on the phone from Dubai. Rita's relative, Indu, has been living in the UAE for the past eight years and last visited her family in Nepal two-and-half years ago. When her mother passed away last April, she had to make an anguished decision: not to come home for the last rites. 'We have good employers, we have good jobs that we want to keep, but we are stuck abroad because of the ban, what is the government doing about us?' she asks.

Unlike others, Nuna, also in Dubai, tried to be less risk-averse and bought her ticket, packed her suitcase, but got cold feet after even the embassy dissuaded her. Nuna has worked with the same employer for three years and wants to continue. 'You cannot imagine how bad I felt while cancelling my ticket,' she says. Thousands of women across the Middle East find themselves in a quandary due to the ban—to visit family and return via India or through 'airport settings'* or to avoid risk and remain abroad till the ban is removed? This is the choice facing many Nepali women, both aspirant as well as current domestic workers. Many are risk averse, while others, whether out of desperation to see their children back home or to land a job abroad that will enable them to take care of their children, find unauthorized ways to get to West Asia, by first going overland to India, or by taking circuitous flights via Sri Lanka. Much of this risk-taking finds its roots in policies that simply don't address ground realities.

The other 'don't-ask-don't-tell' policy that has not been successfully implemented, but policymakers are reluctant to take back is Free Visa Free Ticket. On paper, this sounds like a fantastic proposal because workers should not be paying recruitment costs. This is particularly so, when these costs are borne through informal loans borrowed at high interest rates that take months to repay, thus dampening the benefits of migration. The reality, however, is that migrants are still paying as much as they were, if not more,

---

*When airport employees are also involved. Often, they are paid under the table by recruitment agents to let women pass immigration/security with the wrong visas despite the ban on domestic workers.

but the receipts they are now getting for these payments are of 10,000 Nepalese rupees (US$100) as is legally allowed. This puts both the migrants and the Nepalese government at a disadvantage because, for the former, an accurate receipt is important evidence in case things don't go as planned and, for the latter, the false receipts indicate a loss of tax revenue. Migrants share that they feel uncomfortable with the receipts, but they don't have any option but to accept them. The desperation to go abroad is so high, and the supply of jobs so limited, that recruiters have the bargaining power. They can simply refuse workers who are reluctant to accept the fake receipt. Workers can only hope that 'luck' is on their side and that they won't have to face a situation where they will be required to furnish the receipt as evidence of being defrauded while filing grievances or court cases.

Reducing costs for migrant workers and passing that burden to employers, as envisioned by the Free Visa Free Ticket policy, should of course be the goal. But this policy was implemented without considering the realities of the drivers of the costs or the ability to monitor these costs. Sub-agents arbitrarily charge migrants and there are tens of thousands of such sub-agents across the country; regulating them is extremely difficult. The environment of unhealthy competition between recruiters means that recruiters often pay HR officials or destination-country-based agents for job demand quotas. Nepal's loss is also seen as the gain of another migrant-rich country, such as Bangladesh or Pakistan, where average recruitment costs are two to three times higher than in Nepal. As a result, in this environment of unhealthy competition, it is the migrant worker who ends up bearing the costs of migration. Imposing such policies without considering the root causes of the high costs of recruitment means that they are bound to fail—at the cost of the migrants who, incidentally, are the ones the policies are meant to help the most.

Policies set by the destination country also have the same element of luring migrants to test their luck. Many migrants land jobs that do not pay them as promised or they find that the nature of the tasks are not a good match. Migrants are also often unprepared for and unhappy with their jobs, which often fall in the D3 category (dirty, dangerous and demeaning). But they do not have the option to change jobs legally, no matter how bad their situation is. Rita, a runaway in Malaysia, found out that she would not be getting the overtime that was promised and that she would have to pay other fees as well. For every small mistake at her job in a fish factory, her employer deducted US$15–30 from her salary. She escaped before her contract ended and joined the ranks of the undocumented. With loans adding up back in Nepal, returning prematurely is not an option for many migrants. There is also the pressure of family expectations, as families collectively decide to send members abroad by selling assets or taking loans.

In apartments scattered across cities in Lebanon live many undocumented domestic workers or those who have made 'arrangements' with their Lebanese contacts under which they pay the visa sponsorship fee. Not all employers, especially those without family members or small children in the household, require full time live-in support. Many workers also prefer to live independently. Consequently, they put themselves at risk by living and working in the shadows. 'My Madam refers me to her friends and colleagues so I have enough work every week,' says a part-time Nepali domestic worker. This shadow gig-economy has evolved over time in Lebanon, and often workers get up to US$7 per hour, better than what live-in workers earn. But they live in constant fear of detention by the authorities. There is no legal provision for part-time domestic work in destination countries and when the legal mechanisms don't respond to market needs, it is apparent that underground markets start appearing on their own. As in all other cases, however, workers bear a disproportionate amount of risk while the employers get away with very little retribution even if the workers are caught.

Migrants are very aware about the risks of being caught as undocumented workers; in fact, many have friends who have been caught. This was evident during my trip to Kuala Lumpur when panic spread on the sidewalks of the Kotaraya area as immigration police swept down during one of their raids on undocumented migrant workers. There was palpable fear in the air as those without documents attempted to flee, but were caught and whisked away. When migrants feel stuck, however, they are willing to take their chances and test their luck as undocumented workers, evading police and immigration officials.

There will, of course, always be a certain element of luck and uncertainty in overseas employment, just as in all employment opportunities. In the case of international migration, given the distance and cultural or language barriers, among others, it is certainly stronger. However, in the current scenario, day-to-day decisions are driven by a belief that much of the outcome is out of the hands of the decision-maker, i.e., the migrant. Every aspect of the recruitment process is mired in potential pitfalls for the migrants, with policies that only exacerbate the risks rather than bringing certainty to the process. The more uncertain the environment, or the stricter the migration rules, the more the underground market will flourish, with agents emerging as the heroes: whether those who help migrants navigate the migration process, or those who help cross the borders, or those at the destination who help migrants leave their legal jobs to enter the shadow economy.

Migration-focused policies should do more to reduce the 'unknown' aspect of the process, which makes it akin to a lottery driven by luck—another term for arbitrariness. A good step towards this is to encourage bilateral labour agreements which, though not perfect, address many of the weaknesses discussed above. By involving both the receiving and sending governments, there is more policy coherence such that migrants are not put in a limbo, as is the case with unilateral policies such as Nepal's domestic worker ban or the 'Free Visa Free Ticket' policy. Such bilateral agreements encourage more clarity regarding the costs and more certainty about terms of employment. Some of the better ones, such as the Employment Permit Scheme of South Korea, even allow workers to switch jobs legally up to three times. As a bilateral issue, with migrants living outside the jurisdiction of Nepal, it should not come as a surprise that imposing unilateral policies is bound to fail. To the extent possible, the receiving country should be involved.

At an individual level, migrants are attempting to reduce the uncertainty associated with migration. For example, while agents continue to play a prominent role in migration, conversations with migrants reveal that, unlike in the past when agents were relied upon blindly, migrants have become more careful about selecting agents. One of the parameters used in deciding on an agent, as reported by migrants, is asset ownership. Hira of Dhanusa says, 'We try to get a better understanding of the asset ownership of the agent himself and it is easier for us to trust the more established ones. Agents with lands and houses are tied down and cannot flee to avoid retribution. Their asset ownership signals their ability to return our recruitment costs if our migration attempt fails or if we return prematurely.' Such incidences of agents fleeing were more common in the past. This consideration is in addition to the agent's reputation and the effect of seeing a positive change in the income status and living standard of previous clients. Such informal ways of bringing more certainty to the system, though imperfect, are seen in migration decision-making.

Migration policies should be able to do more to remove the uncertainties surrounding migration. In an ideal world, migration outcomes should have been what economists call a triple win: the destination country gets cheap workers, the sending country's surplus worker problem is solved, and migrants can get employment at a wage differential. However, the 'win' of the migrants is often put to test in a governance system mired with loopholes and incoherent policies. The perception that luck plays a prominent role can make migrants lax about their decision-making, as there is little faith that their being careful or patient has much influence in causing better outcomes. Or, in other cases, the status quo is so abusive and mobility so restricted that the underground economy, with its risks of deportation, seems like a worthwhile gamble. To revisit interventions aimed at making migration systems safe, orderly and regular means a better understanding and targeting of the drivers of these risk-taking behaviours, and going beyond the very generic awareness-related interventions that currently dominate the migration space. With incoherent and restrictive policies in place, generic information alone can often be rendered inadequate, as is reflected in the accounts shared by stranded and rescued migrants. The migration governance system is set up in such a way that even when there are such first-hand exposes of failed migration attempts, other aspirants attribute them more to ill luck or fate, rather than poor decision-making. Unperturbed, they repeat the exact same steps in the hope that in their case the odds will be in their favour.

Notes

1. https://www.fordfoundation.org/ideas/equals-change-blog/posts/why-today-s-migration-crisis-is-an-issue-of-global-economic-inequality; https://www.cgdev.org/sites/default/files/Clemens-Montenegro-Pritchett-Price-Equivalent-Migration-Barriers_CGDWP428.pdf

Human Trafficking from Nepal under the Guise of Foreign Employment

JANAK RAJ SAPKOTA

Introduction

Nepal's National Census of 2011 shows that 40.26 per cent of the population belongs to the 16–40-year-old age group. Yet, despite being eligible for the labour market, this age group lacks employment opportunities inside the country. The Fourteenth Periodic Plan of the National Planning Commission (2016/17 to 2017/18) had planned to increase employment opportunities by 3.2 per cent per year for this age group, but it couldn't manage better than 2.9 per cent in 2016. The Plan also mentioned the fact that although 450,000 Nepali youths enter the job market annually, around 400,000 migrate abroad,[1] especially to the GCC countries. Of the total population interested in taking up jobs in the country (that is, the total population between the ages of fifteen to fifty-nine, excluding those who have migrated for foreign employment), 2.3 per cent remain totally unemployed, whereas another 30 per cent are partially employed. This situation indicates that Nepalis are compelled to migrate in order to find employment, and that the number of Nepalis migrating is consistently increasing due to continued job scarcity inside the country.[2]

The job shortage that compels unemployed youth to migrate out of Nepal also allows migration to flourish through illegal routes. Those operating organized and unorganized human-trafficking rackets lure the jobless by selling big dreams of life and wealth in foreign countries and tapping into the frustration of the unemployed, who are willing to go abroad and earn at any cost. It is evident that the ever-increasing pressure on the Nepali job market, coupled with the tendency to want to make quick money, and the grim spectre of future unemployment in the country, have together been encouraging human trafficking incidents in Nepal.

Human trafficking has long existed in various forms, but the failure to see its presence in connection with modern migration for foreign employment has worsened the situation. The absence of a proper policy and legal system to monitor the conduct of human-resource agency operators and their agents has also nurtured the growth of human trafficking. In some cases, even those who have returned after completing a stint in foreign countries have fallen into the traps of human traffickers, lured by the promise of earning much more money.

According to the 2017 Trafficking in Persons Report released by the US Department of State,[3] Nepal is a source, transit and destination country for men, women and children subjected to forced labour and sex trafficking. 'Nepali women and girls are subjected to sex trafficking in Nepal, India, the Middle East, Asia, and sub-Saharan Africa. Nepali men, women and children are subjected to forced-labour in Nepal, India, the Middle East and Asia in construction sites, factories, mines, domestic work and begging,' it says, adding that manpower agencies or individual employment brokers who engage in fraudulent recruitment practices and impose high fees might facilitate forced labour.

This essay attempts to investigate ongoing human trafficking that occurs under the guise of legal foreign employment. It concentrates on exposing how the tentacles of human trafficking reach into the processes followed for migration and foreign employment, whether through organized or unorganized means. Finally, it also questions whether the weaker policies and regulations that apply to the growing foreign employment sector have been instrumental in allowing human trafficking to flourish in Nepal.

Migration Trends

The migration of nearly 1,200 Nepalis every day has sustained the national economy. A total of 786,636 Nepali workers migrated legally, after seeking valid labour permits from the government agencies, in the fiscal years (FY) 2015–16 and 2016–17.[4] The data also indicate that more than one-third of the country's economy is dependent upon labour migration. Remittances from the foreign employment sector make up the largest share of Nepal's economy.

The remittance inflow to the country was equivalent to 29.52 per cent of the total Gross Domestic Product (GDP) of Nepal in FY 2015–16. This is expected to slump to 24.25 per cent in the FY 2016–17.[5] The contribution of remittances to the country's GDP has been continuously shrinking for the past three years. A decrease in the number of Nepali migrant workers departing for foreign employment after the Gorkha earthquake of 2015, and the greater use of indirect channels to send money from abroad, are possible factors driving the reduction of remittances to the country.

The Nepali government, over the years, has introduced various policies and legal systems to manage and regulate the foreign employment sector. Since the first officially authorized sending abroad of Nepali migrant workers in 1997, the government has endorsed various policy reforms. It first introduced the National Labour Policy in 1999, followed by a separate Foreign Employment Act in 2007 and the formation of the Department of Foreign Employment (DoFE) in 2008 to govern the sector.

The DoFE has listed 108 countries as permitted job destinations for Nepali workers* willing to work abroad, and has given licenses to 752 recruiting agencies to operate foreign-employment bureaus. Despite the government's ongoing measures to regulate the sector, these recruiting agencies and their valid and invalid agents have been involved in illegally collecting excessive charges and exploiting poor migrant workers by various means.

---

*The Nepali government decided to ban workers from migrating to Afghanistan, Libya, Iraq and Syria on 23rd June 2016.

Krishna Neupane, a lawyer with the People's Forum, a non-governmental agency offering free legal services to victims of fraudulent activities, shares[6] that the government's failure to regulate the sector effectively has given rise to human trafficking.

With a growing desire for jobs in foreign countries, and the massive growth of unemployed youth within Nepal, the number of workers migrating through illegal routes is likely to increase. Simultaneously, the unattractive conditions and dearth of decent jobs in destination countries have produced far-reaching consequences: the further migration of job-seekers onwards to fresh countries, via illegal routes secretly operated by organized groups.

Legal Structures

Article 29, sub-article 3 of the Constitution of Nepal, adopted in 2015, states that no one shall be subjected to trafficking or being held in slavery or servitude. Even though the law has recognized human trafficking as a grave crime, the government's efforts in preventing and discouraging the practice have not been effective, which has led to the practice flourishing under the shadows of legal foreign employment.

Sub-section 1 of Section 4 of the Human Trafficking and Transportation (Control) Act, 2007, defines human trafficking as follows:

> If anyone commits any of the following acts, that shall be deemed to have committed human trafficking: (a) To sell or purchase a person for any purpose; (b) To use someone into prostitution, with or without any benefit; (c) To extract human organs except otherwise determined by law; and (d) To go for in prostitution [sic].

Likewise, sub-section 2 of Section 4 of the Act deems the following acts to be human transportation:

> (a) To take a person out of the country for the purpose of buying and selling: (b) To take anyone from his/her home, place of residence or from a person by any means such as enticement, inducement,

misinformation, forgery, tricks, coercion, abduction, hostage, allurement, influence, threat, abuse of power and by means of inducement, fear, threat or coercion to the guardian or custodian and keep him/her into one's custody or take to any place within Nepal or abroad or hand over him/her to somebody else for the purpose of prostitution and exploitation.

While the Act addresses various forms of human trafficking that can exist within the country, it lacks the clarity to recognize the nexus between foreign employment and human trafficking. The existing laws and policies have limited scope in seeing human trafficking as the act of taking the victim to a foreign land, or the roles of agencies set up to regulate the sector in doing so. Even the Foreign Employment Act (2007) has failed to foresee that human trafficking can happen under the name of foreign employment. This Act has been confined to mostly regulating and managing the foreign employment sector, penalizing recruiting agencies and their agents for acting against the law, and controlling cases of fraud.

In contrast, Article 3, paragraph (a) of the United Nations Office on Drugs and Crime makes it clear that human trafficking can include a variety of other actions. In its Protocol to Prevent, Suppress and Punish Trafficking in Persons, it defines Trafficking in Persons as:

the recruitment, transportation, transfer, harbouring or receipt of persons, by means of the threat or use of force or other forms of coercion, of abduction, of fraud, of deception, of the abuse of power or of a position of vulnerability or of the giving or receiving of payments or benefits to achieve the consent of a person having control over another person, for the purpose of exploitation. Exploitation shall include, at a minimum, the exploitation of the prostitution of others or other forms of sexual exploitation, forced labor or services, slavery or practices similar to slavery, servitude or the removal of organs.

Since 2009, both the Acts endorsed for discouraging human trafficking in Nepal—the Human Trafficking and Transportation

(Control) Act and the Foreign Employment Act—have been in force. While the Ministry of Labour, Employment and Social Security shows concern about regulating and managing the foreign employment sector, similar concern is not reflected in the functions of the Ministry of Women, which is mandated to control human trafficking and transportation. Furthermore, the two ministries implementing these Acts have no close coordination between them.

This ambiguity in legal structures has resulted in the categorization of serious human trafficking crimes as mere cases of fraud, further contributing to covering-up such criminal offences. Defects in the legal apparatus have not only made cases appear weaker and deprived victims of justice, but have given an indirect boost to those involved in such illegal activities.

Political Will Required

Government agencies aren't completely unfamiliar with the practice of human trafficking and transportation taking place in the name of foreign employment. The issues have been frequently raised at several meetings of the Parliamentary Committee of International Relations and Labour. Human trafficking, in various forms and manners, however, has continued due to the dearth of serious concern about the matter, lack of strong political will to change the situation, and frequently changing governments.*

On April 2, 2017, a meeting of the Parliamentary Committee had directed the government to find out why human trafficking was occurring and what could be done to discourage the practice. The committee said that despite frequent reports to Nepali missions in countries where the unhindered trafficking of Nepali women was happening, nothing was done to prevent such a grave crime, nor was any interest shown in punishing Nepali and foreign agents involved in the illegal acts. It had also directed the Office of the Prime Minister

---

*Nepal currently has a stable government as two major parties, the UCPN Maoist and UCPN UML, decided to unify as a single party after two major elections—legislative on 26th Nov 2017 and provincial on 7th Dec 2017. Between 2013 and 2018, Nepal saw six government changes.

and Council of Ministers to take action against all those involved, including the Foreign Minister and other senior officials, for not implementing the Directive on Housemaids. The third amendment to the directive in 2016 had banned Nepali women migrants from working as domestic help abroad unless the country had a bilateral labour agreement with Nepal. Nepali diplomatic missions had repeatedly reported back and suggested that the directive had not been fruitful in stopping human trafficking, but instead worked as a legal shield for human traffickers who continued to send women under the guise of foreign employment. The committee report had concluded that Foreign Ministry officials had often pressured diplomatic mission staff to turn a blind eye to the directive, which led to the unchecked continuation of human trafficking.

This shows that neither the government nor the parliament is unaware of the international human trafficking happening from Nepal, but again, the lack of coordination amongst the concerned agencies and the greater political concern about maintaining diplomatic relations with various countries have not resulted in a strong crackdown on the operators.

Deputy Superintendent of Police (DSP) Rajkumar Silwal, who works with the foreign employment pillar of the Central Investigation Bureau of Nepal Police (CIB), says that many fraudulent cases of foreign employment get imbricated with human trading and transportation.[7] However, the combination of lack of evidence, the weak legal structure and powerful agents have prevented human trading under the cover of foreign employment from becoming the central issue.

The Parliamentary Committee is also aware about the ongoing unsatisfactory situation. It said:

> It was found that human traffickers have penetrated deep into the villages and [are] bringing out poor and simple Nepali girls and women to Kathmandu, alluring them by promising good jobs and huge money before supplying them to the UAE, Kuwait and other Gulf countries via the Tribhuwan International Airport and other third-world countries through visit visa or with other channels.

Nepali human traders have set up their own offices in Ajman of the
UAE and Kuwait City of Kuwait for supplying domestic helpers as
if they are selling cattle after selecting among them, according to
Nepali embassy officials and other Nepalis based in those countries.
While the business of trading Nepali women has been going on
openly, the Nepal government has not taken any initiatives for either
deporting them or bringing these traffickers under the jurisdiction
of law. These traffickers seem to have gained protection from high-
level politicians of the country,[8] doubted Nepali foreign mission
officials and representatives from Nepali community.

The Parliamentary Committee confirmed that, without a strong
commitment from high-level political communities and the
government, the daunting task of stopping human trafficking
and transportation cannot be achieved. The government's feeble
commitment towards dealing with the crime, or rehabilitating
trafficking victims, is a major factor behind the unobstructed
continuation of human trafficking.

Problems in Prosecution

The Metropolitan Police Range (MPR) receives at least ten to fifteen
cases of cheating related to foreign employment every day, but the
number of cases related to human trafficking are as low as one or
two per day. The KMPR forwards all cases other than purely cheating
or fraud ones to the DoFE.

The Case Section chief of the MPR, DSP Mohan Thapa, shares
that the confusion amongst victims themselves as to whether they
were traded or just cheated while seeking jobs in foreign countries
has helped to establish the treatment of such cases as general fraud
rather than human trading.[9] He explains, 'In some cases, even after
the victim succeeds in escaping from the clutch of the perpetrator
in foreign countries, where they might have reached through illegal
routes, they only file complaints of fraud. Most of them have no idea
that a case related to human trading can also be registered.'

Thapa further said that although the DoFE rescues victims of
human trafficking, it has not been filing complaints against the

perpetrators, as the Foreign Employment Act has not given the DoFE any authority in such cases. The confinement of the DoFE's role to rescue and compensation recovery has led to the shielding of grave crimes like human trafficking.

When the CIB receives information about women trafficking victims from Nepal who are stranded in various Indian cities, they verify it through various contacts and sources, and then begin their efforts to bring the victims back to Nepal. Between 15 June, 2017 and 17 October, 2017 alone, the CIB rescued eighty-one women trafficking victims from India and other countries. However, they could neither identify the agents involved in the human trade nor arrest any suspects, as none of the victims filed cases against their traffickers. This leads to an abrupt end to the CIB's investigations, without coming to any conclusion. This pattern is common: despite succouring a huge number of victims, security forces have not been able to nab any agents or racketeers involved in these incidents.

Why don't the victims of human trafficking during foreign employment opt for legal remedies? Seeking answers to this question involves exploring the linkages between the existing laws and policies governing the sector and the roles of the government agencies mandated to implement them. The then-CIB spokesperson, Superintendent of Police (SP) Mira Chaudhary, reveals that most victims are sold by their own relatives or someone they know, and those with strong political connections. Rather than filing cases against the perpetrators, victims often drop the idea of going through the complicated legal process, with the decision sometimes influenced by offers put forth to settle the matter and/or possible threats. The victims also don't want to jeopardize their prospects of migrating again. 'Victims have their own obligations and ongoing problems; they start discovering ways to migrate to other countries and earning money anyhow rather than going through the legal procedures involved in filing and pursuing a case against their traffickers.'[10]

According to a DSP associated with the Metropolitan Crime Division, many who have been rescued as victims of human trafficking think of putting an end to the case after getting compensation money, which they often use to migrate again. According to the DSP, the victim has to reach the court and give their statement, which most of them consider an unwanted hassle. They often also refrain from instituting legal proceedings, fearing the harm to their social status once the news about them being sold becomes public.

In the opinion of SP Mira Chaudhary, restructuring existing policies and overseeing human trading is imperative. There is a need for policy clarity to see how human trading takes place under the cover of foreign employment. The police puts forth massive efforts and resources to rescue women who have been victims of such trading, but as those victims don't file cases, the investigation cannot move ahead. With the lack of precision in existing policies and lack of coordination amongst concerned government agencies, the police have no option than to file general cheating cases, even in cases of human trafficking.

In this fashion, an imprecise policy framework and even weaker implementation has given impunity to culprits, allowing human trafficking to continue alongside foreign employment.

Lack of Public Awareness

The NPC's Fourteenth Plan has identified raising awareness about human trafficking and foreign employment as a big challenge.[11] The gap between existing policies and their implementation has created a void in which foreign employment and human trafficking are seen as completely distinct from each other. However, the report indicates that the flourishing of human trafficking alongside foreign employment is a well-known fact among government bodies.

The National Human Rights Commission (NHRC) has defined the practice of forcing labour to work as one of the forms of human trafficking. A NHRC report entitled 'Trafficking in Persons National Report 2015/16' says that forced labour is one of the significant elements of trafficking; and that as migrant workers reach their destinations, they are at higher risk of slipping into the state of forced labour. In such forced labour situations, untimely demise, injuries, mental illness and isolation, separation from the family, abuse and exploitation of migrant workers are widely reported.[12]

Likewise, various studies have shown that excessive economic exploitation, fake promises and coercive agreements by agents have given rise to human trafficking. For example, Amnesty International has reported that recruiting agencies and their agents in Nepal not only charge excessive fees for job placement in foreign countries, but they also exploit poor migrant workers through several means, making them more vulnerable to other forms of exploitation like human trafficking or forced labour.[13] Amnesty's report on sixty-four cases of labour exploitation shows that twenty-two of the workers were victims of human trafficking. It also gave evidence on the direct involvement of recruiting agencies in human trafficking.[14] However, poor understanding of human trading and transportation amongst general society allows these cases to be perceived as merely cases of cheating.

The Alliance Against Trafficking in Woman and Children in Nepal (AATWIN) published a report titled 'Unsafe Migration & Human Trafficking in Nepal: Perception Survey among Communities in Select Earthquake-affected Districts,' in December 2017, saying:

> When asked about their knowledge on human trafficking, only half of the 494 respondents were able to tell one of the constituents of human trafficking, and almost a quarter did not have any knowledge about it. Most of the people interviewed perceived human trafficking as buying or selling of human beings. About a quarter of the interviewees thought that human trafficking was forced prostitution and a small percentage of people thought that it was illegal removal of human organs and voluntary prostitution.

The report has clearly highlighted how the common public has very little understanding of human trafficking and cannot see it as connected with foreign employment. Such confusion further enables human trading to operate unhindered in the name of foreign employment.

Case-by-case Analysis

Nepal's police do not have any data showing how many incidents of human trafficking and transportation are directly related to foreign employment. Even the cases pending in court and under trial that have been filed under the Human Trafficking and Transportation Act are not classified to clearly show whether they involve links to foreign employment. Government data doesn't include sexual harassment, luring for foreign studies, human organ trafficking, foreign employment and other potential reasons as cases of human trafficking. The government also lacks aggregate statistics on the motives behind the trafficking and the sex ratio of the victims.

According to a report of the Crime Information Centre under the Attorney General Office, a total of 227 incidents of human trafficking were recorded in FY 2017–18. The number was lower in FY 2016–17 when only 181 similar cases were reported,[15] but the document failed to give a clear picture of whether the cases were related only to human trafficking or involved human trafficking along with forced detention.

Similar data with the Metropolitan Police Range show that twenty-six cases of human trafficking have been filed from June 15, 2017 to April 13, 2018. The MPR has arrested thirty-one men and six women allegedly involved in human trafficking. The data records twenty-six women as victims, but no corresponding statistics on male victims have been mentioned. According to the police's data, India, the UAE and Kuwait were the destination countries in most cases of human trafficking.

During the same period, thirty-two cases of human trafficking were registered with the CIB. Of the total 101 victims of human trafficking mentioned in these cases, fourteen were women and the remaining were men. The CIB arrested thirty-five accused individuals in response—three women and thirty-two men.

According to top officials with the MPR, while most of the cases received at police stations are about the trafficking of girls for the sex trade in India, the CIB also has a number of cases in which girls were sold after being charged hefty money for study visas in the USA and Europe. The CIB Human Trafficking Cell chief, DSP Rajkumar Silwal, stated that treating cases of human trafficking that occurred during foreign employment purely as foreign employment fraud cases has contributed to creating the present situation.

*

In order to prove that human trafficking and transportation is also linked with foreign employment, this researcher has minutely studied sixteen cases related to human trafficking registered with the MPR and CIB. Of these, thirteen cases have a significant element of foreign employment contributing to the human trafficking. Most of the women victims are illiterate, poor and from downtrodden communities in Nepal. In thirteen cases of human trafficking related to foreign employment, eleven out of sixteen victims are women. Among them, six have had major issues with their families (such as spousal abuse or being widowed); or poor family backgrounds, (e.g.: being orphaned or abandoned) and no education. One woman, who had been sold to a dance bar in Macau, had had a tragic past. Her father had died when she was very young and, as her mother had got re-married, she had been raised as an orphan by relatives. Another woman, traded in Dubai, had the responsibility of single-handedly raising two daughters after her husband died. Without having had the chance to attend school herself, and experiencing extreme poverty, she had seen foreign employment as the last resort to bail herself and her children out of poverty. However, her plan didn't turn out as expected.

Amongst the selected cases, half the victims were found to have reached the destination countries via Indian airports. In eight such cases, it was found that they did not travel via the Tribhuwan International Airport (TIA) in Kathmandu, but went by road across the India–Nepal border. The traffickers then transported these victims to the destination countries through their arrangements with immigration staff at airports in Calcutta, New Delhi and Mumbai.

Some victims had returned from abroad, but planned to go to another country to continue earning money. Three such cases—two women and a man—had returned to Nepal after legally working as migrant workers in Saudi Arabia and Dubai for years. Tempted to earn more money, they fell into the clutches of traffickers, and have ended up losing their earnings from foreign employment.

In other cases, the victims had come into contact with the traffickers through someone they had known during foreign employment.

A woman who had been in Kuwait from 2011, was in touch with another Nepali woman working as a housemaid in Oman. After completing two years of work in Kuwait and returning to Nepal, she met the other lady, who lured her to go to Macau, promising huge earnings. After paying around US$2,466, she got her passport with a tourist visa to Hong Kong. Through the trafficking network spread across Nepal, Hong Kong and Macau, she departed for Hong Kong from TIA on February 25, 2015, where she showed fake documents saying that she would be taking part in a cultural event in Macau. The trafficker took her to Macau via sea. Only after reaching Macau, did she come to know that she had been sold to a dance bar to dance and provide sexual pleasure to clients. Once she realized that she had been sold for sex trading, she ran away from the dance bar and, after a long struggle, managed to return to Nepal, on January 19, 2016, with the help of the Non-residential Nepali Society and Metropolitan Police Crime Division, Kathmandu.

The plight of a woman who was entrapped during a vacation from her housemaid job in Saudi Arabia is even more appalling. While working in Saudi Arabia, she had got to know a Nepali woman there. She met her again in Nepal during her vacation and heard hopeful stories about life in Dubai. They stayed in touch even after she returned to Saudi Arabia. Unhappy with her tough life as a housemaid there, she thought of trying her luck in Dubai and began the process as instructed by this woman. The human trafficking nexus sent her as a regular migrant worker to Dubai via the legal route. Once she landed at Sharjah airport, she was sent to Oman by the agent without her knowledge or consent as she was illiterate. Only when she demanded her salary from her employer after not getting paid for a consecutive seven months, did the employer tell her that he had bought her for US$5,000. After months of suffering the massive work burden, inadequate food, exploitation and physical torture at the hands of the employer, she ran away from the house and reached the Nepali embassy. A further seven months of waiting ensued at the embassy. She eventually returned to Nepal with a travel document issued by the embassy.

Both these cases prove that those who have returned from foreign employment can also be victims of trafficking. In both cases, the traffickers also targetted the hard-earned money of those who have returned from foreign employment. What is even more interesting is the fact that even ex-migrant workers themselves are involved in trafficking. Another case profiled a youth who had returned to Nepal after working in Malaysia, and had pushed a woman into the nexus of traffickers for a few thousand rupees. He succeeded in sending her to Dubai after weaving the plan with his co-worker, whose sister was working there. The trafficked woman could only return after fifteen months of suffering.

Even after returning home from foreign countries, unskilled migrant workers remain deprived of better opportunities in Nepal. The situation makes them dependent on friends and other acquaintances, met during foreign jobs, for further job opportunities and getting in touch with other networks. They then might, in turn, start working for human traffickers as their agents in order to earn money.

Shockingly, in some cases, legally operating recruiting agencies and their agents were found to also be operating as human traffickers. Of the sixteen cases studied, recruiting agencies and their agents were directly or indirectly involved in seven cases.

The story of a woman, originally from Western Rukum, who was sold in Syria for US$7,000, is heart-breaking. She was called to Kathmandu from her rural village to complete the required labour-permit documentation but the agents had used fake documents. After reaching Kathmandu, she was sent to Calcutta via the India–

Nepal border at Kakadbhitta by agents. From Calcutta airport, she was flown to Dubai, from where she was taken to Syria, a war-torn country where the Nepal government has banned* women from going as housemaids.

In her statement, the woman narrated in chilling detail what she had to go through while in Syria. When she asked her employer about the work she would be expected to do, they informed her that she would have to do everything as she had been bought as a slave. If she did not follow their commands, she was beaten. Later, she was sent to different families for household work. Despite the heavy workload, she was only given half pieces of chapatti to eat and, if she couldn't work because of physical weakness, was tortured. As the employer thought she was for his use, he forced her to bed with him every day, which made her fall sick.

The plight of another woman who was sent to Kurdistan is not any less disturbing. She, too, had been called to Kathmandu for legal documentation, and again, the agents had subverted the process using fake documents to send her via legal channels to Dubai. From there, she was trafficked further to Kurdistan. In her statement, she said:

> After reaching the Kurdistan airport at around 10 p.m., they took me to an office through a narrow road, filled with the debris of what looked like a bomb blast or demolition. In the office, there were other five [sic] Nepali women. People would come and select someone they liked among us, as if we were cattle. On the fifth day, they selected me and sent me to my workplace, where I would be working from 6 in the morning till midnight. They would neither provide enough food nor they allowed me any rest. I had to run to their service any moment they would ask. I was never given my salary that I was promised. After three months, they would give me some money, whatever amount they would think appropriate. When I pleaded with them to send me back because of the excessive workload, they told me that they had bought me after paying 13,000

---

*Nepal's Cabinet decided to ban women from going to Afghanistan, Libya, Iraq and Syria as migrant workers on 23 June, 2016.

dollars. They asked me to pay that money before I could leave. Only then I realized that I was sold by the network of traffickers spread from Kathmandu to Syria. I had no other option than to work there.

Legally operating foreign employment has surfaced in the case of both these women. They were trafficked by two different rings, using different routes from Dubai. Likewise, another woman was sent to Dubai by agents, using their set-up in TIA to circumvent the legalities. Even the Parliamentary Committee of International Relations and Labour has pointed out in its report[16] that Nepali women were trafficked to Gulf countries with the involvement of government immigration officers posted at the airport.

Challenges

An ill-managed foreign employment sector and the poor execution of regulations on the part of government agencies have plagued efforts to stem human trafficking. A narrow legal definition of human trafficking and imprecise legal frameworks have also nurtured human trading.

The tendency to view human trafficking and foreign employment as operating through different legal systems has diluted the disturbing fact that human trafficking is operating under the lucrative garb of foreign employment. Even more alarmingly, this appears guided by the ill-intentions of traffickers, who target the most vulnerable groups, like the unemployed and women. As human trafficking is run smoothly under the legal cover of foreign employment, and the hiring for foreign jobs is undertaken by recruiting agencies having massive political backing, the crime has remained unabated.

The biggest hurdle in dealing with human trafficking cases is starting legal procedures once the victim is rescued. Unless the victim files a written statement in the court, clearly stating that she or he was traded, the police cannot move further, resulting in a situation where most human trafficking cases remain outside the legal setup.

In one instance on May 4, 2017, the CIB rescued forty-four women who had been halted at the immigration check-post in

Dubai airport. The unsuspecting women had first reached New Delhi, India from Nepal and taken a flight to Dubai from there, believing that they were headed to Kuwait for domestic work. Police later concluded that traffickers had intended to take them to Kuwait through an illegal route, and traffick them there. Each of the women had paid their agents Nepali Rs 100,000–150,000 (US$1,000–1,050) to land employment in Kuwait. Despite being cheated and nearly sold as slaves, all of the women decided to keep it quiet. They neither named their agents nor filed complaints. As a result, the CIB could not continue their investigation, despite seeing clear evidence of human trafficking on such a large scale.

Despite being rescued from the jaws of trafficking, the women still had a strong determination to work abroad. 'Dreams of women who have faced severe financial crunch or domestic violence revolve around the dreams peddled by agents while promising foreign jobs. They do not wish to file cases against their agents, even though they had intended to sell them,' said Chaudhary, adding that this lack of awareness and co-operation from the victims makes it difficult to take action against human trafficking networks.

This seeming impunity that human trafficking networks enjoy has fuelled their confidence, as well as sent a message to victims that they are not entitled to justice in the existing legal framework.

On their part, human trafficking agents have been taking full advantage of the government's failure to properly regulate the sector. Those who are illiterate, poor and have little knowledge of the foreign employment sector easily fall into the trap of these trafficking rackets.

Poor awareness regarding human trafficking, whether amongst policy makers, police, the legal fraternity, aspiring migrants or society in general, has sustained international trafficking in persons in various forms. The Fourteenth Plan of the NPC lists[17] the government's efforts to curtail human trading and transportation. The NPC has tried to study the problem and seen the links between human trafficking and foreign jobs, concluding that raising awareness about foreign employment and human trafficking is a major challenge.

Conclusion

As Nepal's economy has been largely dependent upon remittances sent by its migrant workers, foreign employment has become a significant sector for the country over the years. Recruiting agencies responsible for hiring and placement of migrant workers have become a dominant force in the country. They enjoy massive political support—a large number of such agencies are either owned by influential individuals or have been backed by someone in power. Also, as these manpower companies have been the source of indirect funding for political parties and have even formed wings of mainstream political parties, they have remained untouched by law and order to a large extent.

A narrow definition of human trafficking that has completely ignored the possibilities of the crime going under the garb of foreign employment, a vague legal system, coupled with the reluctance of victims to file cases and of the concerned bodies to see the practice as more than merely fraud, have further sustained the human trafficking.

A ministry or department for combating human trafficking is needed. The regulation of agents must begin at the village level, the weakest link in the recruitment process. Stronger enforcement of the Foreign Employment Act (FEA) of 2007 is imperative, including harsh punishments for perpetrators.

To date, the discourse on the connection between migration and human trafficking is poorly developed, which has hampered efforts to improve the situation and may have exacerbated the problem.[18]

The Human Trafficking and Transportation (Control) Act has a limited definition of human trafficking. The Act has recognized any act of human selling and buying as human trafficking, but has not acknowledged that such trade is possible during foreign employment. Likewise, the Foreign Employment Act 2007 has said that the migrant worker cannot be forced to work against their will by threats of any kind: economical, physical or psychological. But it has again failed to relate such force with human trafficking. It has become imperative to widen the definition of human trafficking by incorporating fake promises, use of illegal routes for reaching destination countries, forced labour and other tortures.

The Nepal Police and government lawyers involved in the investigation and prosecution of human trafficking also need to understand the entire trafficking ecosystem in depth. For this, the government needs to develop policies with utmost clarity. Likewise, government bodies regulating the foreign employment sector should also be alert and expand their activities beyond fraud to investigate exploitation in the sector and explore how human trafficking is flourishing alongside foreign employment.

Finally, reform in existing policies and legal systems, a separate body for overseeing human trafficking cases and a strong database to keep track of those involved will help greatly in discouraging the ongoing practice of human trafficking.

Notes

1. 14th Plan (fiscal year 2074/75/76). National Planning Commission. Government of Nepal.
2. Ibid.
3. https://www.state.gov/j/tip/rls/tiprpt/
4. Labor Migration for Employment: A status report (2015/16–2016/17)
5. National Audit Information, fiscal year 2074/75. Central Bureau of Statistics. Government of Nepal.
6. Interview with Krishna Neupane (25th March 2017).
7. An interview with DSP Rajkumar Silwal on 4th May 2018.
8. A ground-zero monitoring report of Gulf countries prepared by sub-committee formed dated 08 Mansir 2073 under the Parliamentary Committee of International Relations and Labour.
9. An interview with DSP Mohan Thapa on 16th May 2018.
10. An interview with SP Mira Chaudhary on 25th October 2017.
11. https://www.npc.gov.np/images/category/14th-plan-full-document.pdf
12. http://www.nhrcnepal.org/nhrc_new/doc/newsletter/397604438 Trafficking_in_Persons_National_Report_2013-15.pdf
13. Maanislai munafama parinat garidai (*Making men into profit*). Amnesty International. 2017.

14 . Maanislai munafama parinat garidai (*Making men into profit*). Amnesty International. 2017.

15. Yearly report 2074 by the Attorney General's office, that includes crime analysis.

16. A ground-zero monitoring report of Gulf countries prepared by sub-committee formed dated 08 Mansir 2073 under the Parliamentary Committee of International Relations and Labour.

17. https://www.npc.gov.np/images/category/14th-plan-full-document. pdf

18. Labor Brokerage and Trafficking of Nepali Migrant Workers VERITE, Fair Labor worldwide, https://www.verite.org/wp-content/ uploads/2016/11/Humanity-United-Nepal-Trafficking-Report-Final_1.pdf

A Return to Nothingness

R.K. RADHAKRISHNAN

The sight of anxious relatives waiting to greet their loved ones outside the arrival gates is quite common at most Indian airports. Many happy faces dot the more than 2,200 flights that transport people between India and the Gulf Cooperation Council (GCC) countries, either heading out to what is widely believed in India to be the land of opportunities, or returning home with an assortment of gifts. Not all homecomings are happy though.

Barriers After Death

In 2016, as many as 3,380 workers who had left India to seek a better future for themselves and their families abroad, came back in body bags. A majority of these Indian workers had died in West Asia: Saudi Arabia (1,559), UAE (825), Kuwait (295), Oman (272), Qatar (152) and Bahrain (107). The only other country which recorded Indian worker deaths in the three digits in 2016 was Malaysia, with 170.

Sending a body back home is easier said than done. If the employer does not diligently follow the procedures and paperwork, this process needs considerable support from the Indian Mission and local non-governmental organizations working for the welfare of migrant labourers. In some cases, the employer bails out of sending the body home; in others, the labourer had been working for a contractor who is not obliged to send the body back; and in a few others, the labourer was an irregular—without the correct visa for employment.

Take the case of Ilango Perumal, a driver from Paramagudi, Tamil Nadu, who died of a heart attack on May 5, 2018, in Doha, Qatar. The hospital he was taken to, the Hamad Medical Corporation, said in its report that the direct cause of death was 'recent thrombus occlusion of Left Anterior Descending Coronary (LAD)' and listed it as a natural death. Almost a week after the death, his distressed family still did not have information about why his body's return had been delayed. Ilango's mother, Vijayalakshmi, petitioned the District Collector (DC), the highest authority at that level, taking help from the local Member of Parliament, Anwar Razza.

The normal progression of such a petition is from the DC to the state headquarters in Chennai, from where it will be routed to the Public Department. The Tamil Nadu government sends this petition to Delhi, where it reaches the External Affairs Ministry finally, for further action.

On enquiring with the DC's office and the Indian Embassy in Qatar about the delay in the release of Ilango's body, this writer came to know that the No Objection Certificate from the Qatar police was pending. This certificate could only be given to a representative of Ilango's company, once they approached the police.

The intervention of a Member of Parliament, Kanimozhi, who happened to be in Doha at that time, and the help of the Indian Ambassador to Qatar, P. Kumaran, as well as that of the local Tamil Sangam in Qatar, helped process the case quicker than usual. Ilango's employer, who was an employee of the police department, was willing to bear the cost of flying the body back, with two attendants. The twenty-four-year-old's body was flown back just ten days after the various people began the process of helping out.

While death is inevitable, the paperwork that follows—a requirement for bringing a body back to India—is excruciatingly painful. There are a host of certificates to be obtained, first in the country of death, and then at the local airport where the body lands. To get the required certificates from the local Mission, a list of papers need to be submitted. These include: the passport/civil identity card of the deceased, a death report issued by the hospital authorities/mortuary, the civil identity card of the person intimating the Indian Embassy of the death and a letter from the employer. Once these have been submitted, the Embassy/Mission will give the list of documentation required for further processing. These include buying an air-ticket, sealing the coffin, and an embalming certificate in triplicate. The embalming certificate is normally in Arabic. When it is handed over to the local diplomatic mission, the medical practitioner attached to the mission will translate it to English. A copy of this must be handed over to the airline carrying the body.

More processes await the next of kin once the body reaches India. The airport's health post, the police, the airline and the immigration department—all are involved in formalities before the body can be claimed. Finally, the body has to be claimed from the cargo terminal, which is always a few kilometres from the passenger terminals. Unlike the friendly passenger terminals, most cargo terminals in India barely have any information kiosks as they are usually frequented only by regulars. This is where the touts come in. For a steep price, which differs based on what services are required, they offer to get the body out.

For a barely-literate relative, none of these processes are decipherable. Laden coffins lying in cargo terminals for weeks on end are not a new phenomenon for many Indian airports, according to a Customs officer in Chennai who once helped a family retrieve a relative's body.

Distressed Homecomings

Indian workers, who left their homes hoping for a better future in the 'Gulf' (a popular term used to refer to all GCC countries) have been coming back home involuntarily for a variety of reasons. On a Monday night in October 2017, this writer spent time at Chennai's Anna International Airport to witness one of the most depressing sights: the homecoming of a few deported Indian nationals. As many as four were from Malaysia, one, quite strangely, from Japan, one each from Sri Lanka and Dubai. All of them were labourers looking to make it past the immigration controls in the 'wrong' countries. There are countries, mostly in West Asia, where the immigration officials allow a migrant worker on a tourist visa to enter even though it is very apparent that the person was not there for any tourism-related activity. But most countries in Southeast Asia, and the Far East, Australia and New Zealand keep a close watch on who is being let in. In the agent's book, these are 'wrong countries.'

Three more landed in Chennai with emergency travel papers issued by Indian Missions abroad. These were migrant labourers, who on landing, and clearing immigration, found that they had been cheated. Their passports were collected by the host sent to meet them, and they were taken to an accommodation. After a few days of inactivity, their 'host' vanished. According to their accounts on reaching Chennai, the three took different routes to the nearest Indian Mission—in one case, the labourer was lucky that a conscientious person asked him what was wrong, and guided him; in the second case, the labourer was found dumped in front of an Indian Mission; and in the third, a diplomat had spotted the labourer, hailed a cab, and paid him to get to the Mission. Issuing emergency travel papers, for those who have lost their passports, has risen to the status of a full-time job in at least ten missions in West Asia.

The same day, at the departure terminal, two women were off-loaded for not receiving clearance from the Protector of Emigration, the office tasked with certifying migrant labourers going abroad after ascertaining the details of their job with the employer. The job of the Protector, as the name suggests, is to ensure that the migrating labourer is not duped once he or she lands in a foreign country.

What happens to a person who has been deported or was denied boarding by the Indian Immigration? 'Only very few take it as fate, go back and never return,' says an immigration officer at the Delhi Airport. 'Most will come back and try their luck again. They manage to get through, provided there is no remark against their names and if all their travel papers are ok,' he adds.

One manpower agent, who spoke on the condition of anonymity

in Chennai, said that it was always possible to circumvent immigration officials. 'Some shifts have strict officers. Some shifts have officers who think, why should we stand in the way of someone trying to make a living? We know who these people are,' he said. A lot depends on the top immigration official too. If she or he concentrates more on people who are entering the country than those who are leaving, the task of the agent is much simpler. Also, if the officials in one airport are tough, the agents switch to a nearby airport because most cities have good connections to all West Asian destinations.

Some Indian migrant labourers have used general amnesties announced by governments in the GCC to return home, as an alternative to deportation. The Kuwait government's amnesty, which waived fines for those who overstayed their visas, and a similar Saudi Arabian amnesty, attracted a large number of Indians who had been working in irregular low-paid jobs.

Of the Indian expatriate community of 950,000 in Kuwait, as many as 27,000 were 'residency violators.' As many as 15,000 took advantage of the offer. In Saudi Arabia, 75,952 Indian nationals came forward during the campaign period (March 29, 2017 to November 14, 2017).[1] During this 'Nation Free of Violators' campaign, Indian Missions issued 32,960 emergency certificates, gratis, so that labourers without passports could travel back to India. After the expiry of the amnesty, the Saudi government began a campaign of arresting and summarily deporting undocumented expatriates. As many as 6,000 Indians were forced to leave under this campaign.

Another category of distressed returning workers is that of those injured in the course of their work or by their employer, usually returning with next to nothing. Some, like fifty-eight-year-old Kasthuri Munirathinam, a domestic worker from Vellore, Tamil Nadu, had been tortured in Saudi Arabia. She had a hand cut off in 2015 before she managed to get free of her employer. This is not an isolated incident. Sister Lissy Joseph of the Hyderabad-based National Workers Movement has a file full of the various examples of exploitation and abuse that domestic workers undergo abroad.

Kasthuri's agonizing stay in Saudi Arabia makes for a particularly horrible nightmare. According to Kasthuri, unable to bear the treatment she received as a domestic worker, she had attempted to leave the third-floor apartment by climbing down from a window using a rope made from a sari. She was accosted by the woman she worked for just before she managed to escape. Kasthuri said, 'I pleaded with her not to harm me, but she kicked me, punched me and cut off my arm.'

This was not all. Saudi Arabian authorities, taken aback by the Indian response—a strong statement asking for action against the employer—changed tack. The Riyadh police claimed that Kasthuri was 'mentally disturbed,' while making no mention of the allegations of brutality and torture against the employers that led to her attempt to flee. Soon after this aggressive Saudi response, the Indian authorities piped down, and refused to counter the claims of the Riyadh police. The Saudi Embassy in New Delhi joined in as well, distributing statements to the national press that repeated the Riyadh police's claim that Kasthuri's arm had been severed when she 'lost her balance and fell down, hitting the edge of an electricity generator located on the lower part of the house.'[2]

Once she landed in Chennai, Kasthuri was admitted to Tamil Nadu's biggest public sector hospital, the Rajiv Gandhi Government General Hospital. According to officials, she was not found to have any psychiatric illness, barring the trauma-induced problems. The Chief Minister of Tamil Nadu at the time, Jayalalithaa, sanctioned 1,000,000 Indian rupees (US$13,614) for her. In a press note, the Chief Minister said that the amount would be invested in a government entity, and the interest accruing each month would be given to Kasthuri.[3]

*

Workers might lose their jobs and have to return due to larger forces as well, such as conflicts in the destination countries or a surge in nationalist sentiment, leading to a loss of employment.

Conflict Rescues: Government's Pride

Governments love numbers because these give a certain veneer of credibility to their intentions more effectively than sweeping policy talk. So, it was with justifiable pride that India's External Affairs Minister, Sushma Swaraj, said on May 31, 2018,[4] that the country had 'safely evacuated more than 90,000 people from foreign countries' and that, 'on the basis of the strength of friendship developed by our Prime Minister with the rulers of other countries, we got released hundreds of people from the jails. Some have been released from the trap of [the] gallows and some have been brought back after their huge penalties were forgiven.' The minister made these remarks to highlight the achievements of India's four-year-old Narendra Modi government, which was stepping into a general election year.

The Ministry of External Affairs (MEA) said that many of those rescued through government intervention were manual labourers. The well-to-do often find a way to leave long before the first hints of trouble become a full-blown crisis. It is those who prefer to wait it out—because they do not have the means or capacity to flee— who become victims, unless they are rescued by a friendly force or government.

Ensuring the safety of Indians, especially the most vulnerable migrant labourers, is an uphill task. For instance, India reacted as soon as the Islamic State of Iraq and As-Sham (ISIS) captured large swathes of Iraq beginning in June 2014. A travel advisory was issued on June 15, 2014, and all Indian nationals were advised to avoid all travel to Iraq until further notification. The MEA reported that Indian Missions in Iraq assisted 7,195 nationals to travel back to India, including providing/facilitating air tickets to 6,195 workers.

Yemen's political troubles since September 2014 led to India putting together 'Operation Raahat,' the code name for the evacuation of Indian nationals from that country. A total of 4,743 Indians and 1,947 foreign nationals from forty-eight countries were evacuated till April 2015. In May 2018, as many as thirty-eight Indians stranded in Yemen after a cyclone hit Socorta Islands were rescued by the Indian Navy.

A similar exercise in Libya was launched in August 2014, and as many as 3,710 Indian nationals, out of an estimated 6,000 were evacuated. The Indian Mission in Libya also managed to secure the release of six Indian nationals who were being held in captivity by the ISIS. After South Sudan became a theatre of war, India launched 'Operation Sankat Mochan' on July 14–15, 2016, and rescued 153 Indians and two Nepali citizens.

Each of these operations has been undertaken by Government of India at a significant cost, during a period of heightened conflict, to ensure the safety and security of its citizens. But two instances of Indian migrants refusing to flee the host country throw light on an aspect that has been overlooked in each of these rescue missions—the need for a sustainable livelihood for the affected soon after they land on Indian shores.

While the operation to rescue Indians in Libya was underway, as many as 1,750 Indians refused to avail themselves of the facility, despite the Government of India issuing as many as eighteen advisories. One MEA official who was part of the team that led the rescue, told this writer that those who decided not to come back did so because they had nothing left in India. 'Some of them have been in Libya through the bombings of Gaddafi's palace in 1986, and the actions of the Western powers later. They think that this too will pass, and that stability will return,' he said. But the main reason was that 'They feared beginning life all over again in a land that they no longer knew.' That 'new land' for them was India.

A similar situation was witnessed in South Sudan. *The Hindu* reported on July 14, 2016:

At one point when the first C17 stopped at Kampala, Uganda, for refuelling on its way back to India, Secretary (Economic Relations) Amar Sinha announced on Twitter, 'Till last night 300 wanted to leave. Half changed their mind this morning.'[5]

Nearly half of those who had signed up for rescue had changed their minds even before this:

Even as it sent two C17 aircraft with a team under the leadership of Minister of State for External Affairs V.K. Singh, to evacuate hundreds of Indians caught in the civil war in South Sudan, officials ran out of patience as many changed their decision to leave at the last moment. As the aircraft landed, officials faced an unprecedented challenge when nearly half of the 600 Indian nationals declined the offer to be evacuated, citing the ceasefire which has brought a welcome break after a week of intense fighting.

Workforce Nationalization

From the mid-90s onwards, the large number of immigrants in GCC countries has often impelled these countries to think about replacing some of the migrant workers with its own citizens. The United Arab Emirates, Saudi Arabia and Oman are among the countries that have led the nationalization initiative because they saw the writing on the wall when it comes to the GCC's countries' hitherto unquestioned monopoly over oil.

Youth unemployment in GCC countries appears to be the main reason spurring nationalist sentiments in employment policies: in Kuwait, unemployment has jumped from 3.0 per cent (1991) to 15.5 per cent (2017) according to World Bank figures;[6] in Oman from 48.0 per cent to 48.2 per cent during the same period; in Saudi Arabia from 29.6 per cent to 34.7 per cent; and in the UAE from 4.6 per cent to 5.1 per cent. Across the Arab world, World Bank data for the same period points to only a minor dip in youth unemployment—from an unacceptable 27.9 per cent to a similarly unacceptable 27.3 per cent.

The nationalization drive in Saudi Arabia was propelled by the fact that over 300,000 Saudi graduates were jobless and that 130,000 graduates are added to the job pool each year, according to the *Saudi Gazette*. The government, under pressure to act swiftly, apart from cracking down on irregular workers, has made it impossible for migrants to bring their families to live with them. Beginning July 1, 2017, an expatriate worker has to pay 1,200 Saudi riyals (US$320) a year for each member of the family. Till now, the tax was merely

100 riyals (US$26.66) a year for the whole family. About 3,000,000 Indians live and work in Saudi Arabia.

'Over three years, the kingdom has been aggressively implementing the Nitaqat nationalisation programme, with industries replacing foreign workers with Saudi youths. Wages have come down sharply for expatriates', says K.P.M. Basheer, writing about the issue in *The Hindu*, on July 7, 2017.[7] He adds:

> The Saudi General Authority for Statistics estimates that there are one crore [100,000,000] expatriate workers in the kingdom and 24 lakh [2,400,000] dependents. The expatriates' dependents are now being viewed as a huge burden on the economy and one estimate claims that each expatriate costs the government roughly 1,500 riyals [US$400] a month in terms of subsidies on water, electricity, gas and other essentials.

The situation for migrant workers in Oman is taking a turn for the worse because of its nationalization drive—a move towards more employment for its citizens. Saleh Al Shaibany wrote in *The National* on March 10, 2018:[8]

> Oman announced it would create 25,000 new jobs for its nationals between December 2017 and the middle of 2018, in an effort to reduce unemployment as the country experiences its worst job crisis in 40 years. According to the Ministry of Manpower nearly 60,000 Omanis, mostly graduates, are looking for work.

The March 10 report titled 'Oman nationalization drive threatens thousands of expats' jobs' claims that:

> The aim has been to create 40,000 to 50,000 jobs each year for the next five years—half of them in the private sector and the other half in the public one. But over the last two months, the Ministry of Manpower has sent lists of unemployed Omanis to private companies, asking them to replace their expatriate staff members for local ones.

As oil prices remain volatile, and the educated population in West Asian countries increases, more and more foreign workers will be replaced by the citizens of these countries, leading to a foreseeable increase in the numbers of migrants returning to India.

Lost Jobs, Unpaid Salaries, Uncertain Futures

For workers who have lost their jobs or been cheated of their wages, the journey back home is accompanied by uncertainty about the future. The feelings of nostalgia and romance that usually accompany homecoming are replaced by heightened anxiety and palpable tension.

Many migrant labourers coming back home have lost their jobs and not received their salaries, in some cases for many months. In August 2017, two batches of workers from a company in Oman landed in Hyderabad and Visakhapatnam, after struggling for months without salaries. Their stories are similar: despite not receiving salaries for a few months, they continued working, hoping that the salaries and back wages would be given soon. When this did not happen, the workers were unable to manage. In this case, eighteen persons from Itchapuram, Andhra Pradesh, did not receive their salaries for more than four months. It was after this, and with the support of local Telugu organizations that the workers approached the Indian Mission, which helped them return to India. As many as fifty others landed in Hyderabad in August 2017. In all, as many as 800 labourers were rendered jobless and penniless after the company shut down.

This is not an isolated case. A note from the MEA made available to the Parliamentary Standing Committee in 2017 says,

> There are some reports of retrenchment of Indian workers and loss of jobs resulting from closure of companies as well as premature termination of existing contracts. Instances of unpaid dues/ salaries have been reported from Kuwait, Qatar, Saudi Arabia and Oman in recent months. Kuwaiti authorities have imposed a hike in [rates in] availing medical treatment, charges for obtaining residency, etc., in respect of expatriate workers. The recent GCC crisis involving Qatar has created financial pressure on companies undertaking infrastructure projects and may have potential adverse consequences for Indian workers.

Landing and After

In all the above scenarios, rescuing migrant workers from conflict or distress situations, getting the paperwork done to allow them to board a flight to India, and ensuring their safety in the interim is the responsibility of the MEA. But the questions begin to mount once these rescued persons reach Indian airports. In most cases, government intervention ends there.

In the case of those who landed at Hyderabad from Muscat, one local NGO persuaded the state government to give them some cash so that they could reach their homes, further in the interior of the state. 'It was just a gesture on the part of the state government. We suggested and they came forward to help,' said M. Bheem Reddy, vice president, Migrants Rights Council, an organization that provides pre-departure awareness to those leaving abroad for employment. It also helps those in distress abroad, in partnership with the Indian Missions and other NGOs.

What happens to those coming back to India after they lose their jobs? Reddy says:

> This was not a new phenomenon. Labourers have been coming back for the last twenty-five years... But the problem is that there is no return and reintegration programme by Government of India or by the state governments. There is no clear-cut policy for rehabilitation. When the people are coming from Gulf, they have skills. While going, they might have just gone as labourers. But when they come back, they are coming with some skills and experience. Sometimes they also have some money too. If the government provides some support, they will be gainfully employed and we can provide some jobs to them such as plumbers, masons, and electricians. The government should give some institutional support.

An Incomplete Homecoming

While the Government of India could take pride in bringing back 90,000 persons, the question remains whether it can convince their former employers in alien lands to give them their back wages. Invariably, before a company shuts down or before the onset of a conflict, wages have not been paid for several months.

Reddy says:

> Many people come back with empty hands […] The Indian Embassy
> can file cases in the labour court for the recovery of the wages.
> These migrant labourers can give power of attorney to the Indian
> Embassy and it should take care of the court proceedings. This is
> very important. The affected party, a migrant labourer, will not be
> able to stay on in a foreign country and fight a court battle. They are
> also not in a position to engage an advocate. So the Indian Embassy
> could help them with legal aid. There have been cases where the
> labourer comes back and commits suicide because there is a debt
> which they are not able to pay back.

On average, about 5,000 workers die in foreign countries each year.
'The government does not give them an ex-gratia,' Reddy points out.
Many of them have worked for years, sending or bringing substantial
amounts of foreign exchange to India. Reddy feels that this entitles
them to some government consideration. 'It is their right,' he says,
adding that those sending back huge amounts of money to India are
not white-collar workers in Europe and the US; a vast majority are
poor labourers from West Asia. 'So should it not be a responsibility
of the State and Central governments to look after them?'

Non-resident Indians remitted US$69 billion to India in 2017,
says a World Bank estimate,[9] topping China, whose residents sent
back US$64 billion the same year.

The Kerala Model

One of the more organized returnee rehabilitation schemes is that of
Kerala, from where a large number of people migrate every year to
work in the Gulf. According to the state government, there are about
2,200,000 international migrant workers hailing from Kerala, of
whom as much as 90 per cent are in the GCC. The state government
set up the Department of Non-resident Keralite's Affairs (NORKA)
in 1996—the first such state body in India.

While the model has shortcomings, there is no parallel at
this scale worthy of study, barring one from the Philippines. The
Kerala Government's rehabilitation package, NDPREM (NORKA

Department Project for Returned Emigrants), brings together all stakeholders and helps the displaced person make an informed choice. Under this scheme NORKA Roots ,which is the field agency of Norka, entered into Memoranda of Understanding with several major banks, namely State Bank of India, South Indian Bank and Union Bank. According to the Kerala government's website, the Kerala State Backward Classes Development Corporation and Kerala State Pravasi Welfare Development Co-operative Society [PRAVASIS Ltd.] have also signed an MoU and are associating themselves with the project.

The primary working factor in this is that the nationalized banks sanction loans for starting modest enterprises to the returned Keralites. NORKA Roots releases a capital subsidy of 15 per cent of the project cost (up to a maximum of 2,000,000 Indian rupees [US$27,228]) and an interest subsidy of 3 per cent for the first four years, to those beneficiaries who do not default on payment. In case of defaults, the benefit can be availed only if the beneficiaries clear any outstanding dues. NORKA Roots also conducts orientation and training camps prior to screening and selection to inculcate managerial capabilities in entrepreneurs.

Another crucially important facility provided by NORKA is the issuing of identity cards to those from Kerala working outside the country. The identity card can be filled up in the local language, Malayalam, since most migrant workers will not be conversant with English. Once the application is verified, the individual gets an identity card, and the government of Kerala gets data on where a particular Non-resident Keralite is located, which is useful both while they remain overseas and when they return.

Returning migrants can also register their bio-data on the NORKA Roots website, which also has a database of experienced persons in foreign countries. Job-seekers can register to connect with jobs overseas or in India, if they are returning. Around 31,000 people have already registered in the site.

Another service that NORKA offers Non-resident Keralites abroad is the identification of credible NGOs working towards the welfare of Keralite migrant labourers in the destination countries.

NORKA Roots has identified forty-seven credible NGOs in the UAE, Saudi Arabia, Bahrain, Kuwait, Brunei, Israel, Australia and the United Kingdom, the majority being in the Gulf countries. If there are repeated issues with any such organization, NORKA cancels the recognition awarded to the NGO and puts up a public notice on its website.

On June 27, 2018, Kerala Chief Minister Pinarayi Vijayan, offered to help the over-worked and under-staffed Indian Embassies in the GCC. 'If the External Affairs Ministry permits, Kerala is prepared to open NORKA cells in Indian Embassies in countries where there is a large population of Keralities,' he told the Press Trust of India, a widely trusted Indian wire agency. This is easier said than done because the same kind of demand could be voiced by many other states of the Indian union. There is also the possibility of turf wars breaking out at multiple levels because the External Affairs Ministry is the agency tasked with the welfare of Non-resident Indians in general. Questions will be raised on the need for another agency in the embassies, when the issue is the brief of the External Affairs Ministry.

The Impossibility of Return?

NORKA is merely a single state organization that assists returnees. But although elected representatives and the Government of India are aware of the issues faced by returnees, not much else has been done. A question about the problems faced by migrant workers upon their return to India was raised by a member of the Standing Committee on External Affairs in early 2018. In response, the MEA said that the government had launched a State Outreach Programme (Videsh Sampark series) from May 2017 to generate awareness at a state level, and that resettlement and rehabilitation would be taken up at a higher level during conferences held by this programme. The reality is that returning migrants face many challenges. The MEA has itself identified some of the problems, including the inability of states to absorb the returnees and offer employment because of the already high unemployment rate. The economic and employment situation in many states is also not strong enough to introduce social programmes and sociocultural reintegration of the returnees. The lack of state-government-level systems that can guide returning migrants in an integrated and comprehensive manner is a serious concern. It is evident that all the systems in place are not geared to help a barely-literate migrant labourer, and there are no options for soft loans or financial benefits that prioritize returning blue-collar migrants.

This situation forces many a migrant labourer to remain in the destination country, even if the conditions there are less than favourable. The woes of the returning migrant workers invariably get back to others in the GCC, due to the strong bonds that migrants develop with the other workers that they have stayed and worked with for years. Many that I spoke to decided that it is better to just wait out a few more years in their current situations, given the uncertain job scenario back in India.

After a long chat with a security guard in Ras al Khaimah, where he repeatedly complained about the working conditions, I asked him why he did not think of going back home. 'Yes, I would like to go back. Yes, I am not happy with what I go through here. There is nothing much that I can do back home to get a comparable salary. So, I'm just hanging on for just this year to make a small cushion for my family,' he said in all earnestness.

His colleague, who was within earshot, walked over and asked me: 'Did he tell you he was going back?' I nodded. 'Yes sir, we all do that. In fact, we all want to return,' he replied. 'But just as we think of winding up here, there will be something needed back home. And you know the conditions back home. So where is the option of going back?'

He nodded at the first security guard. 'You think he will go back next year?' he asked me.

I remember telling him that I did not have a clue.

He laughed, and called the guard over. 'Tell him how many years you have been telling us that you are going back next year!'

We all laughed. I bought my bottle of Chivas Regal and left.

Notes

1. http://gulfbusiness.com/saudi-extends-amnesty-campaign-one-month/
2. https://www.thehindu.com/news/international/saudi-police-try-to-shift-blame-on-indian-maid/article7771306.ece
3. https://www.india.com/news/india/jayalalithaa-announces-rs-10-lakh-aid-for-hand-severed-maid-691150/
4. https://www.mea.gov.in/media-briefings.htm?dtl/29927/Annual_Press_Conference_by_EAM_on_completion_of_4_Years_of_Government_Translation_May_28_2018
5. https://www.thehindu.com/news/national/300-Indians-decline-airlift-from-South-Sudan/article14488707.ece
6. http://web.worldbank.org/archive/website01418/WEB/0__C-301.HTM
7. https://www.thehindu.com/news/national/kerala/tax-forces-indian-families-to-exit-saudi/article19226671.ece
8. https://www.thenational.ae/world/gcc/oman-nationalisation-drive-threatens-thousands-of-expats-jobs-1.711912
9. https://www.indiatoday.in/india/story/india-largest-remittance-receiving-country-in-the-world-report-1232619-2018-05-13

Returning Migrants Demand Policy Changes in Pakistan

HANIYA JAVED

For Iftikhar Ahmed in Riyadh, Saudi Arabia, much of 2017 passed in anxiety. There were times when the forty-year-old from Azad Kashmir, Pakistan, didn't have any money for food or to make a call home to his family. His experience was not an isolated one. Ahmed, along with 300 others from India, Pakistan and the Philippines, had been waiting since 2016 for his salary to be cleared. Their employer, Empower Contracting, a subsidiary of Bin Laden group, shut its operations, but for some of the employees, salaries had been outstanding for months beforehand. Videos shared by Ahmed would often show the employees protesting with placards outside embassies and labour courts.

It all began at the start of 2016, when the biggest builders of Saudi Arabia, the Bin Laden Group and Saudi Oger Limited, went bankrupt, as a result of which thousands of employees were laid off. For Ahmad and his fellow employees of Empower Contracting, a subsidiary of the Bin Laden Group, it meant a delay in salaries, with some not being paid for as long as eleven months.

Around November 2017, with the exception of three workers, the company cleared the salaries of all Pakistani workers. Thirty-one Indian workers still continued to struggle for their share. For Ahmad, this wasn't the end of the ordeal, as it took him another few weeks to get an exit stamp on his passport and leave for Pakistan.

Five months later, it is peak summer in Pakistan, with urban centres reeling from the effects of an unforgiving sun. Coupled with the heat, it is Ramzan, when the Muslim world fasts for a month. Speaking over the phone from Azad Kashmir, Ahmad however, sounds undeterred. 'I did receive an offer from a Saudi-based German company for mechanical foremanship just recently. It didn't work out because of visa issues,' he says. 'I've been unemployed for many months. The only jobs you get here are [paying] 15,000 to 20,000 Pakistani rupees a month [US$112–150]. How can a household survive on this salary?' he asks. 'I can't afford to set up any business as it needs some capital to rely on as backup. I have no such arrangement.'

For the same salary, Ajmal Ahmed is feeding his wife and five children. 'I'm able to provide my kids with two meals a day working at a loom, if power outages don't ruin the day. I'm happy here. I became poor when I went to Saudi Arabia,' he says.

Ajmal spent a year and a half in Makkah and never, in his wildest dreams, does he want to go back to Saudi Arabia for work. During his first one-and-a-half months there, starting February 2016, Ajmal would hide in his room. 'We had no iqama [residence permit], so it wasn't safe to even step out. I would have nothing to eat,' he recalls. 'In my contract, I was signed as a plumber but I was taken for masonry most of the time. Iqama was supposed to be given by the company along with visa but this didn't happen. I gave 300 riyals [US$80] from my own pocket for it,' he said. 'In all my eighteen months of stay there, I worked only five to six months. The rest of the time I was in my room.'

'I wouldn't call home for months. I had nothing to say about why I wasn't sending money. On top of that I had to pay 300 riyals [US$80] every month to my visa owner. When I couldn't pay him for a couple of months, he would blackmail me and tell me he would have me blacklisted from the sponsor. I was promised I'd get work for 100 riyals daily [US$26.66], but ended up doing it for 50 to 60 riyals [US$13–16] when I had no other option,' said Ajmal.

For Ajmal, the entire thing was a lie from the very start. According to him, a certain Mian Ghafoor, a well-known personality in his village in Faisalabad was sending a few workers abroad when Ajmal requested him to include him as well. 'He told me once you will get to Saudi Arabia, you will be able to send 40,000 Pakistani rupees [about US$299] back home; that is, after deducting my own personal expenses. I was also told that the company would bear my lodging. Nothing of this sort happened. I had no place to stay. In fact, I had no job at all other than masonry here and there for two weeks at most. I had paid Ghafoor 350,000 Pakistani rupees [US$2,618] for the visa, paid for my own passport, ticket and medical.'

In his scattered work regimen, Ajmal can recall one place where he worked for a month and was paid nothing. At another place, he was signed up for 130 riyals a day [US$35], of which he was paid 80 riyals [US$21], and the rest would go in his contractor's pocket. 'I worked with this particular employer for two months and three weeks, got fed up and stopped going to work. The contractor bullied me and said he wouldn't pay me for all the months I had worked if I didn't come for work. He swore at me,' said Ajmal. 'All together, I got 600 riyals [US$160] out of that job.'

Ajmal wanted to leave Saudi Arabia together with twenty-one others, but the visa agent would neither end the contract nor let them be free. 'We couldn't chase the agent on our own because we didn't have visa for Jeddah,' he said. But help did come for Ajmal and two other Pakistani workers. An old acquaintance of his was friends with a local who had connections with the police. According to Ajmal, the police called the agent in Jeddah and told him he had five hours to get to Makkah with the passports of the three men. Ajmal's friend gave the three men some money and they made it to Pakistan. He left 175,000 Pakistani rupees [US$1,309] worth of unpaid salary behind.

Abid Hussain, now twenty-two years old, spent a year and a half in Saudi Arabia as well, and came back with five months of salary. 'The total pending salary was of nine months. My employer paid me five months of it, through which I bought my ticket to Pakistan and never looked back,' he said.

'One of my cousins had told me about an agency in Faisalabad that was sending some men to Saudi Arabia. I got a visa and was happy to go. I got stuck there as soon as I landed.'

For Hussain and hundreds of other Pakistanis it was common to hear that the company had no money to pay to its employees. 'The food was on us and not being paid on time meant no money for anything. I couldn't pay for my mobile bill,' he said.

There were many times when Hussain and others would try to get in touch with the agency in Faisalabad who sent them to Saudi Arabia. The agent would tell them to wait and he would do something. In November 2017, Hussain came back to Pakistan with forty others. Hussain visited the agent's office. 'He was no longer there in his office. I got to know that he left for Malaysia. Someone else sits in his chair now,' said Hussain.

Iftikhar, Ajmal and Abid are examples of thousands of Pakistani workers from Saudi Arabia who have been forced to come back home due to a variety of reasons.

Saudi Arabia: From Most-preferred Destination to Most-exited Country

Saudi Arabia has historically been the most sought-after destination for Pakistani migrant workers. This was equally true for more than a million Asian migrant workers, according to the Asian Development Bank's latest report, 'Labor Migration in Asia'.[1] This changed in 2016.

The drop in emigration from Pakistan to Saudi Arabia between 2016 and 2017 was 41 per cent. The decline was most noticeable starting September 2016. The Bureau of Emigration & Overseas Employment[2], a government body that oversees migration in Pakistan, explains that at this time Pakistani workers (along with Indian and Filipino workers) were restricted to camps owned by companies as many were unpaid. They didn't have enough money to travel home or stay through legal means in Saudi Arabia.

'The drop observed in 2016 can be related to the country's economic situation, as well as to the ongoing "Saudization" policy, first introduced in 2011, which aims at reducing foreign worker reliance,' the Labor Migration in Asia report concurs.

Although there is no specific data available on the numbers of returning migrants, it was reported that Saudi Arabia sent back around 40,000 Pakistani workers towards the end of 2016.

In the first half of 2017, that is, between January to June, only 77,600 Pakistani migrants went to Saudi Arabia in comparison to 233,287 in 2016, marking a decline of 75 per cent. The Bureau of Emigration explains that the emigration decline to Saudi Arabia is the most substantial amongst the GCC countries.

'Pakistan is bearing the brunt of the slowdown of the Saudi economy in terms of export of manpower, as Saudi Arabia is the largest source destination country for Pakistani diaspora,' states the mid-year (Jan–Jun) 2017 analysis report of the Bureau of Emigration & Overseas Employment.[3] The almost 50 per cent decline is most significant in the skilled, semi-skilled and unskilled categories* of labour migration, as these are engaged in construction work. 'It indicates that Saudi Arabia's cut in its development budget affected the construction sector's projects,' states the report.

Changes in Saudi Arabia's employment trends appear to be multifold. As is evident through Iftikhar's story and the Bin Laden Group's bankruptcy, the public department, responsible for most of the construction projects in the kingdom, delayed their payments for government contracts. The Bureau of Emigration & Overseas Employment further analyzes that the decline in oil prices in turn affected the transport and infrastructure budget of the kingdom by 63 per cent in 2016. The low revenue generation from oil companies affected the labour industry, consequently affecting the livelihood of Pakistani workers, many of whom were engaged in construction and infrastructure projects. The Asian Development Bank writes:

Labor migration from Pakistan also declined 11% in 2016 to 840,000 people after it had reached a peak year in 2015. This

---

*The other possible categories defined by the Pakistani government are Highly Qualified and Highly Skilled.

downward trend is likely to continue into 2017 since partial
figures up to October indicate only 450,000 departures for overseas
employment from Pakistan.[4]

Workers who recently returned to Pakistan complain about lack of
consistency in their work. Either the proposed project could not
continue due to lack of funds or what was promised to workers was
not what they got when they reached Saudi Arabia. 'I was signed
up for plumbing but did everything. The contractor would take us
on a project and we would work for fifteen to twenty days and then
we were back in our rooms waiting for work for weeks,' says Ajmal
from Faisalabad.

Despite the drop in emigration, the largest number of migrant
workers to Saudi Arabia in 2016 continued to be from Pakistan.
Over 460,000 citizens of Pakistan followed this route that year,
which represents an 11 per cent drop. In 2017, however, Bangladesh
appears to have replaced Pakistan as the main labour provider to
Saudi Arabia, reflecting changing trends in Saudi Arabia's approach
to Pakistani labour.[5]

Ajmal, who stayed until 2017, felt that Pakistani workers are
increasingly being discriminated against. 'During the times we all
would wait for work, contractors would hire Indian and Bangladeshi
workers and take them for work. They were also able to acquire a
second iqama [residence permit] after the first one expired in a
year,' he said.

There is a common feeling among Pakistani workers that since
workers of other nationalities tend to settle for lower daily wages,
companies prefer to employ them. 'Our [Pakistani] economy has
been going down and the currency conversion doesn't help us. How
much should one keep for personal use and what to send to family
back home?' said one worker.

As per numerous media sources, half a million Pakistanis were
deported between 2012 and 2017, half of which (about 280,052)
were from Saudi Arabia. The figures indicate an increasing trend
in deportation from Saudi Arabia, starting in 2012 with 17,369

Pakistani workers being deported, 45,456 in 2014 and going all the way up to 57,784 in 2016. The reasons for deportation are said to be overstaying visas, illegal entry and immigration.

As many as 39,000 Pakistani workers were deported between the end of 2016 and February 2017.[6] The Saudi media reported that a number of Pakistani nationals were involved with the Islamic State (IS). A few were also held for drug trafficking, forgery and physical theft. The *Saudi Gazette*[7] also reported that the kingdom's security forces had intercepted a terrorist operation in 2016 in which two Pakistanis, a Syrian and a Sudanese national were found planning terrorist activity at Al-Jawhara stadium in Jeddah. More than 60,000 spectators were present at the stadium to watch a match between the Kingdom of Saudi Arabia and the United Arab Emirates. 'The terrorists had booby-trapped trucks loaded with 400 kg of explosives,' according to the *Saudi Gazette*.

In 2015, when crisis hit the Bin Laden Group, and the employees of Empower Contracting weren't paid for three months, they decided to go on a strike. For Zulfiqar Hussain, a thirty-two-year-old resident of Rawalpindi, six more months went in waiting. His health insurance began to expire and savings were fast running out for him and fifty other Pakistanis. 'I resigned but it wasn't the end for me. We waited another ten months for money and gratuity settlement and to simply get our exit from the kingdom.' According to Hussain, 80 per cent of those who initiated the strike were Pakistani nationals. Hussain has spent seven years in Saudi Arabia as a mechanical supervisor and thinks Pakistani workers are the first ones to speak against any violation of rights. 'Even in small companies, the smallest of problems will be called out by Pakistanis first. They are eyed as trouble-triggers often.'

The shift in Saudi Arabia, from being the largest importer of Pakistani labour, to now reporting high numbers of deportations and voluntary returns, leaves Pakistan in a murky situation.

Remittance Reduction and Its Results

The return of migrants in huge numbers raises a lot of questions, not only about their settlement and employment, but also on how Pakistan's economy is to bear the remittance gap. From January to April 2018, 122,917 workers migrated from Pakistan, as compared to 496,286 during the whole of 2017. Consequently, remittances to Pakistan also saw a steep drop in the last two years. For the fiscal year 2016–17, overseas Pakistanis sent US\$9.46 billion, down 2.27 per cent from US\$9.68 billion in the previous year.[8]

Saudi Arabia and the UAE host the bulk of the Pakistani labour force abroad, and hence send the most remittances back to Pakistan. Remittances from Saudi Arabia alone faced a fall of 6.62 per cent in FY 2016–17. As of now (i.e. the fiscal year which runs from July 2017 to April 2018), the State Bank of Pakistan states a -9.46 growth for 2018, since migrant workers are still the largest source of remittances to the country, despite the decline in numbers.[9]

The results of these aggregate declines bear all too human a face. As the head of the family, with two young siblings and five children to look after, Ajmal thought selling his plot of land to emigrate was a justified gamble: the money would be recouped in the coming days. He moved his family to a rented house, sold his plot and made the visa and ticket arrangements, which cost him around 200,000 Pakistani rupees [US\$1,496]. His wife was expecting their fifth child when Ajmal left for Makkah. After two months in Saudi Arabia with no work prospects in sight, Ajmal started getting anxious. 'I hadn't sent a single penny home. My wife was due. They were very difficult days.'

One of Ajmal's younger brothers was working and bringing in about 10,000 to 12,000 Pakistani rupees [US\$75–90] every month. That's what the entire household relied on, but the rent remained a worry for the family. A year later, Ajmal's wife, children and siblings were told by the landlord to leave the house. They had failed to pay any rent during that time.

While Iftikhar Ahmed was suffering in Riyadh, there were repercussions at his home in Rawalpindi too. His brother had taken it upon himself to take care of Ahmed's wife and daughter who studied in fourth grade. 'I think about him and it worries me a lot. We are making it by somehow, but does he have food to eat? How is he living without any money?' said Ahmed's brother. The family also once took a loan from another brother in Bahrain to get by, as many times they wouldn't have any food at home.

The constant devaluation of the Pakistani rupee against the US dollar spurs inflation in the country. In June 2018, the Pakistani rupee dropped by 9.5 per cent against the dollar, reaching a whopping 124.50 rupees to the dollar in the open market. In instances like this, when reserves are constantly relied upon to stabilize such market fluctuations, remittances play a vital role.

'The context for return migration to Pakistan is thus characterized by, on the one hand, instability, and on the other, future potential. It is also a context where there is substantial reliance on remittances, disproportionate to the number of international migrants,' indicates a 2015 policy brief by Peace Research Institute Oslo (PRIO).[10]

For this reason, Pakistan not only needs to invest in a clearer and effective migration policy, but also needs to have an expansive approach. It needs to look beyond Saudi Arabia and UAE as its only key sources of remittances and regulate migration to other countries too.

Future Prospects in GCC Countries

The Bureau of Emigration & Overseas Employment explains that the emigration decline to Saudi Arabia is the most substantial amongst the destination countries for Pakistani workers. However, while Saudi Arabia noticed a decline of 48 per cent in overall labour recipients between January to June 2017, other Gulf countries observed a decrease too. A comparison shows that emigration to the UAE was only down 6.27 per cent and to Bahrain 4.41 per cent over the same period, while Oman decreased by 3.75 per cent in comparison to 2016.

The future prospects are generally bleak. Oman is said to have several developmental projects, such as the construction of hospitals, airports and malls, in process. However, according to the Bureau of Emigration, Oman is only taking in migrants as per the designated proportion for these developmental projects and, like Saudi Arabia, its long-term plan is to employ Omani nationals in both private and public sectors. In the foreseeable future, jobs for Pakistanis are going to reduce in Oman as well.

Similarly, despite being the hub of trade routes and attracting a considerable number of Pakistanis, Bahrain has reduced the number of Pakistani migrants it employs. However, the country intends to start a few developmental projects in oil, gas and infrastructure, which may encourage migrant worker employment in the near future.

On the other hand, Kuwait showed an increase of 56 per cent in labour absorption from Pakistan. The Bureau of Emigration shares that it is the semi-skilled and skilled worker categories that are the most in demand in Kuwait. 'It is expected that the demand for highly qualified and highly skilled manpower will increase in the forthcoming year,' states its 2016 report.[11]

Qatar, too, showed a 20 per cent increase in the number of Pakistani migrants last year. Mass development is happening in Qatar as part of its Vision 2030 plan. Pakistanis employed there are mostly on the technical side of construction and development projects. Despite garnering a great deal of media attention in the last four years owing to the human-rights violations reported against migrant workers, Qatar is still a thriving destination for migrant workers.

Given the growing trend of returning labour from its most preferred destination countries, Pakistan needs to ask itself some hard questions. How does the country plan to absorb this high number of returnees, and what is the future of these skilled and semi-skilled labourers?

Employment Prospects in Pakistan

The Pakistan Bureau of Statistics, a government body that records demographics, records unemployment as well. For example, only 34 per cent of people coming from sales and service backgrounds show employment across rural and urban sectors in 2013–14. Taking into account that this figure is from five years ago and that there are likely to be more unemployed personnel in the near future, considering the number of people returning from major labour destinations abroad, the question of how each province of Pakistan plans to deal with this problem becomes urgent.

Pakistani Demographics

The Population Council published a report in August 2016[12] titled, 'Youth in Pakistan: Priorities, realities and policy responses' in which it said that among the fifty-four Commonwealth countries, Pakistan ranks twenty-second in the Commonwealth Youth Development Index (YDI). The YDI is a composite index based on education, health, well-being, employment, civic and political participation.

Pakistan has one of the lowest employment rates, and the numbers consequently show substantial migration. According to the report, more than seven million Pakistanis travelled overseas for employment through the Bureau of Emigration & Overseas Employment between 1971 and 2013. About 96 per cent of this manpower goes to GCC countries, with Saudi Arabia being the most preferred destination, followed by the UAE.

'About 50 per cent of these migrants are aged 15–24. This makes it crucial for Pakistan to have in place a solid and clear policy for supporting overseas employment for Pakistani youth,' says the 2016 report.

In any of the GCC countries, one comes across female migrant workers from India, Nepal, Bangladesh and Sri Lanka, in the domestic and other sectors. Where are the Pakistani women?

Pakistani women make up only 0.21 per cent of Pakistani migrant workers abroad, according to a study by the International Labor Organisation.[13] However, the vast majority of women migrate internally, from rural to urban areas. On the surface, there seem to be no legal barriers against women's employment abroad, other than an age restriction of thirty-five years for domestic workers.

This is to avoid instances of abuse and trafficking. One sees no clear government policies encouraging women workers to go abroad.

It is interesting to note where the bulk of this negligible 0.21 per cent go. Between 2008 and 2013, 6,444 women went abroad, out of which 3,860 (60 per cent) went to the UAE and almost 18 per cent went to Saudi Arabia. While on the one hand, there's the question of lack of encouragement and legislation for female migration, on the other, there's the dilemma that arises from the migrant destinations: the migration trend for both male and female migrants in Pakistan is centred towards the UAE and Saudi Arabia—both of which are facing a decline in demand for migrant labour.

The Need for a New Migration Policy

Labour migration is not a new phenomenon for Pakistan. It has seen its high moments in the 1980s, specifically when it comes to migration to Saudi Arabia. What is lacking is a solid migration policy crafted by the state.

'The main emphasis of (the government) targeting overseas Pakistanis has been increasing remittances, specifically the proportion sent through the formal banking system,' writes Marta Bivand Erdal, a senior researcher at PRIO. In her analysis, Erdel considers the scope of governance in Pakistan. She argues that limiting governing capacity at national, regional and local levels negatively impacts both the development and implementation of migration policy. She writes:

> People's generally low levels of trust in government and public institutions are a challenge for governance, including of return migration. Pakistan is a country of emigration, transit and immigration. But as for many other states, there are severe constraints on the state's control over migration. Given the multiplicity of return migration to Pakistan, coupled with weaknesses in the state's capacity to perform governance nationally and locally, the dilemmas remain largely unaddressed. Conversely, the potential for socioeconomic development—including as a positive by-product of migration—stays untapped and deprives Pakistani society.

One would think that after bearing so much, both financially and emotionally, a worker would want to return to his home country at the first given opportunity. But this doesn't appear to be the case for many Pakistani migrants. When workers wait for months for their dues to be cleared, some think of sticking around a little longer, in case they find a better alternative job.

Jadoon, for example, doesn't plan to return to Pakistan, if he can avoid it. He's a survivor of the financial crisis that hit the Bin Laden Group and forced thousands of Pakistani migrant workers to return home, giving up salaries worth years of service. At the peak of the crisis, another subsidiary of the Bin Laden Group offered him a job and he decided to go for it. 'I thought going back and starting from scratch would be more difficult for me,' says the thirty-six-year-old who went to Saudi Arabia when he was twenty-five. 'I thought it was better that I remain on duty and recover my previous dues that were still pending with the company.'

As of now, Jadoon is still waiting for six months' worth of salary from previous years, while his iqama stands expired. 'I mostly stay in my compound and if the police catches us on the way or back from duty, the company is responsible for us then. Between 2015 and 2018, the situation has improved a lot,' he says.

'I don't plan on going to Pakistan anytime soon. You see, Saudi Arabia has nothing but oil and we [Pakistan] have everything and yet we spend our lives like slaves of our political system.'

Given the lack of political stability and a depleting economy, those who return to Pakistan still want to migrate again and start afresh, if they can afford to. As such, there is no incentive for returning overseas migrants, unless they have some savings to rely on until they find work or start a small business on their own. For instance, Zulfiqar Ahmed, a mechanical supervisor who had also waited ten months for his salary settlement in Saudi Arabia, works as a daily wager in Pakistan, earning 500 Pakistani rupees a day (US$4). He can't wait to go back to the GCC for a better opportunity. In his group of forty-five other Pakistanis, some went to the UAE, while others went to Qatar and found work there.

Even those like Iftikhar, who suffered the worst kind of mistreatment—bearing appendicitis pain for months, having no money for food or to call home, spending their days protesting outside on the roads—would still go back to Saudi Arabia or any other destination abroad, given the opportunity.

The lack of employment opportunities in Pakistan, as the system has no policy or emerging strategy to absorb the returning pool of migrant workers, paints a bleak picture for those contemplating a return. 'How […] can a worker manage in the meagre income you get in your home country? There is no value of hard work here. With the way the rupee is devaluing, how can we survive here [in Pakistan]?' asks Zulfiqar.

Notes

1. https://www.adb.org/sites/default/files/publication/410791/adbi-labor-migration-asia.pdf
2. https://beoe.gov.pk/files/statistics/yearly-reports/2016/8.pdf; https://beoe.gov.pk/files/statistics/yearly-reports/2017/2017-full.pdf
3. https://beoe.gov.pk/files/statistics/yearly-reports/2017/2017.pdf
4. https://www.adb.org/sites/default/files/publication/410791/adbi-labor-migration-asia.pdf
5. http://saudigazette.com.sa/article/172517/39000-Pakistanis-deported-in-4-months
6. http://saudigazette.com.sa/article/172517/39000-Pakistanis-deported-in-4-months
7. http://www.saudigazette.com.sa/article/166292
8. https://beoe.gov.pk/files/statistics/yearly-reports/2017/2017-full.pdf.
9. https://fp.brecorder.com/2018/01/20180122337530/
10. Erdal, M.B. (2015) Pakistan as a Return Migration Destination, PRIO Policy Brief, 13.
11. https://beoe.gov.pk/files/statistics/yearly-reports/2016/3.pdf
12. https://www.popcouncil.org/uploads/pdfs/2016PGY_YouthInPakistan.pdf
13. https://www.ilo.org/islamabad/info/public/pr/WCMS_625357/lang--en/index.htm

Pakistan's Forgotten Workers on Death Row

SABRINA TOPPA

I. Zulfiqar Ali

Indonesia

Wrapped in a green hospital gown, a plastic tube inserted into his nostrils, Zulfiqar Ali knew that his last days were upon him. He had arrived in Batu Prison on Nusakambangan island—darkly referred to as 'Execution Island' by the Javanese—with dim prospects of survival. In May 2018, his wan face seemed expressionless, lying still and frozen on the hospital bed.

Spending thirteen years on death row had left Ali in a perennial limbo since 2004, unsure about the passage of time. In 2016, Indonesia had ordered Ali to face death by a firing squad after convicting him of drug possession, despite a dearth of evidence. Back then, with a mere seventy-two hours remaining until Ali faced his executioners, Pakistan's then prime minister, Nawaz Sharif, had directly intervened, taking the rare step of imploring the Indonesian government to grant clemency to a Pakistani migrant worker.[1]

However, almost two years later, there was no grand intercession by the government of Pakistan when Ali's health began to fail. At fifty-four years old, Ali heaved his last breath, succumbing to the last stages of liver cancer in the intensive care unit of the jail's hospital. Despite the plea by the Pakistani prime minister, his name was still firmly lodged in Indonesia's database of drug convicts when he died.

*

In 2001, Ali had left behind work in a textile mill on the plains of Punjab, Pakistan's largest and most fertile province, and arrived in Jakarta to stake out a new fortune. He had settled down, married an Indonesian woman named Siti, and fathered five children. By all accounts, his life was on the upswing, propelled forward by a job as a marketing manager at a friend's company. In his free time, he tended to a side business, supplying Islamic garments manufactured in countries like Pakistan to the Indonesian market. Fortune seemed to favour him in these early days, and he was able to acquire three homes spread between Pakistan and Indonesia.

Despite his rapidly increasing prosperity and blossoming familial roots in Indonesia, Ali's social and cultural ties to the country were still somewhat tenuous. His command of the Bahasa Indonesian language remained weak, and he largely fraternized with South Asians. It was through these circles that he made the ill-fated acquaintance of an Indian migrant worker named Gurdip Singh in Jakarta.

In November 2004, this connection would cost him gravely, when Singh was stopped by Indonesian authorities at Jakarta's main international airport for carrying 300 grammes of heroin, a crime punishable by death in the country.

At the time, Ali, then thirty-eight, was staying at his house in Bogor, enjoying the cooler temperatures of a city set against the once-volcanic Mount Salak. Ali had no awareness of Singh's movements at the airport, nor of the drugs he had in his possession, his lawyers say. That did not impact the ensuing events. Policemen soon knocked on Ali's door in Bogor and handcuffed him, claiming that his name had surfaced during their questioning of Singh. The police believed he was involved in the drug smuggling.

Despite proclaiming his innocence, Ali was hauled away by officials to an unknown house, where he was beaten by the police over a three-day period to extract a confession. During the thrashings, the police—who had entered Ali's home without a warrant—said they would kill him if he did not sign the confession paper. Fearful of what might result if he did not assent to their demand, Ali placed his signature on the paper, effectively signing his life away.

He ended up spending seventeen days at a police hospital for kidney and stomach surgery. According to Ali's lawyers, he never recovered from some of the injuries sustained during the torture.

Although Ali was alarmed at Singh's accusation that he was involved in drug smuggling, there was one scrap of news that brightened his mood: Ali learned that in a court affidavit, Singh had recanted his earlier statements that the drugs were Ali's, confessing that the police had encouraged him to list someone else's name in order to reduce his own punishment.

However, despite Singh's statement, Ali was not freed; he still had to stand trial. Ali stumbled through the courtroom proceedings with a dim grasp of the Bahasa Indonesian and English being spoken, almost entirely reliant on his interpreter's translations. His mother tongue was Urdu, and both English and Bahasa Indonesian were second languages Ali had little mastery of. Adding to Ali's problems was the fact that he did not have a lawyer. A month after his trial had started in 2005, Ali received a lawyer, but by then it was too late. Despite a lack of evidence showing that Ali had brought any drugs to Indonesia, the Tangerang District Court sentenced him to death in June 2005.

Ali was told that the punishment would be execution, but he could serve a lesser punishment of ten to fifteen years in prison if he simply paid a 400 million Indonesian rupiah bribe, equivalent to US$27,762 at the time. Ali refused to pay the extortionate sum, declaring himself innocent.

Ali filed an appeal two months later that was rejected the following year. Despite the setback, Ali nonetheless pursued his case all the way to the Supreme Court, which struck down his request to overturn the punishment in 2008, upholding his original death sentence.

In 2010, after news surfaced that Ali faced trial without a lawyer and with subpar translation assistance, Indonesia's ex-president

Susilo Bambang Yudhoyono ordered an inquiry into Ali's case. The inquiry declared that Ali was innocent and, going one step further, acknowledged that he had suffered custodial abuse at the hands of the police. Despite this good news, Ali's fate did not change—the inquiry's findings never made their way into the courtroom proceedings.

In April 2013, Ali filed a case review to re-examine the case. Noting that Ali had no prior drug history or convictions, lawyers argued that Ali's case had multiple deficiencies—not only had he been operating without a proper interpreter, there was no evidence that he had committed the crime, a particularly egregious oversight in light of the severity of the punishment.

However, his case review was rejected on unknown grounds, and in July 2016, Ali received the dreaded order: in seventy-two hours, the Indonesians would execute him by firing squad. By August, the Justice Project Pakistan (JPP), an NGO assisting Pakistanis on death row, launched a vigorous media campaign that drew attention to Ali's case. Through the JPP's efforts, the case reached the highest echelons of power in Pakistan, prompting then-Prime Minister Nawaz Sharif to call upon Indonesia to halt the execution.

The Indonesians responded favourably, swiftly placing a stay on the execution. However, they did not acquit him of the charges and he still faced the death penalty at a later date. Part of the problem was that the Tangerang District Court still deemed Ali's confession—obtained through police torture—valid in the court of law. His lawyers were outraged; not only were there no drugs found on Ali when he was taken by the police, the relatively minor quantity of heroin Singh had been carrying when he implicated Ali simply did not match the gravity of the punishment. In other cases, heroin possession of far greater quantities had yielded milder punishments.

Complicating matters was Ali's health which, by December 2017, had deteriorated entirely. That month, Ali's physician informed him that he was suffering from stage-4 terminal liver cancer that doctors had no cure for. The likelihood of him dying—either on death row or in the hospital—was now almost a foregone conclusion. His lawyers pleaded with the Indonesian government to grant him clemency and release him for medical reasons, repeatedly underlining the fact that authorities had no evidence that Ali had carried heroin into Indonesia in the first place.

Importantly, Ali gravely needed a liver transplant, though the operation was expected to fail. Mounting medical costs threatened his physical health, as doctors discovered additional illnesses ranging from cirrhosis of the liver to diabetes. To pay the bills, Ali and his family sold his houses, and eventually Pakistan's Ministry of Foreign Affairs paid more than US$37,000 to cover his medical bills. This did not solve the larger imbroglio. Medical staff told Ali he only had a few months to live at best, and those would likely be spent in a jail hospital.

Nonetheless, a faint hope arose in January 2018, as an opportunity for an appeal opened up. The country's highest authority, the Indonesian president, was one of the few officials empowered to pardon a prisoner, and president Joko Widodo was making a rare state visit Pakistan, during which he planned to sign memoranda of understanding with his Pakistani counterpart and even address the parliament in Islamabad. According to then-foreign minister Khawaja Asif, during Widodo's highly-publicized meeting with prime minister Shahid Khaqan Abbasi, the latter directly implored Widodo to release Ali on medical grounds.[2] For its part, the JPP, the main NGO working on Ali's case, swiftly seized the opportunity to organize a media campaign around Zulfiqar Ali's case. The appeals seemed to work; Widodo himself promised to reconsider the case during his visit, a drastic reversal from a man who had once told Indonesian media he would never grant clemency requests for drug trafficking. Widodo 'had declared war against drug traffickers, pointing to the increasing number of drug abuse victims,' said Justice Minister Yasonna. '[He] was not planning to abolish capital punishment anytime soon, particularly in cases of drug trafficking,' according to a December 2014 press release.[3]

Yet Widodo's promise remained unfulfilled. This might have owed partly to the fact that it was never followed up on by Pakistan's own foreign ministry, says Rimmel Mohydin, the former head of communications at the JPP.

*

Today, more than 11,000 Pakistanis are detained in jails around the world, many being migrants grasping at economic opportunities abroad to escape political and financial instability at home. The country lacks a consular protection policy for citizens detained abroad, a fact that has major ramifications for migrant workers. Typically, a consular protection policy establishes a range of services to citizens facing distress or detention abroad, ranging from legal representation to visits to jails by consular staff. 'It appears that the government has adopted a policy of "no policy" on overseas Pakistanis,' said Lahore High Court's chief justice Syed Mansoor Ali Shah, during a 2017 court hearing of a lawsuit filed by the families of migrant workers on death row.[4]

In Ali's case, the Ministry of Foreign Affairs was alerted by the JPP to his ordeal. Given his ill health, both the NGO and his family asked Indonesia to repatriate Ali, but this never materialized. According to the JPP, the Pakistani government's negligence played a role in Ali's death in Indonesia. Under Article 4(1) of the Pakistani constitution, the government holds a responsibility to protect citizens, which the foreign ministry patently failed to carry out by not advocating for Ali's repatriation.

Indeed, although the interventions of both prime ministers Abbasi and Sharif demonstrated Pakistan's capacity to impact how its migrant workers fare abroad, this pressure is rarely exerted. Instead, inaction by government institutions, and particularly Pakistan's foreign service, is far more typical.

II. Abu Zar

Saudi Arabia

Like Zulfiqar Ali, Abu Zar was a Pakistani migrant waiting for a response that never came from his government. In February 2012, Abu Zar was excited for his first trip home to Pakistan in two years, paid for by the Al-Sagheer taxi company that employed him in Saudi Arabia. His days were spent driving, for wages much higher than he could command back home in Pakistan's Bhakkar district, an expanse of verdant land situated in the eastern province of Punjab.

After Abu Zar's customary trip home that year, which involved greeting relatives, lavishing them with gifts, and enjoying his own joyful reprieve from the toil of driving, Abu Zar's family drove him nearly five hours north to Islamabad airport. There, they embraced him for the final farewell.

After the routine goodbyes, the family expected Abu Zar to immediately embark on the plane for the onward journey. However, unbeknownst to them, an old colleague from Al-Sagheer had contacted Abu Zar, seeking help with a mundane task. The request was simple enough: Abu Zar was asked to carry an extra luggage item on behalf of the colleague, to be delivered to family in Saudi Arabia. Abu Zar agreed without asking what was inside the bag.

Abu Zar proceeded through passport check and the security gate without any problems. At the time, he was distracted by thoughts of his family—he knew he wouldn't see them for another year or two.

When the plane descended at Jeddah airport, however, Abu Zar's situation changed radically. Almost immediately after landing, Saudi airport security informed him that they had discovered drugs in his luggage. Unbeknownst to him, the tyres and handle of the bag he had taken from his colleague were lined with illicit narcotics.

The response was swift: Abu Zar was arrested for drug possession and immediately transported to Briman prison in Saudi Arabia's western quarter. For at least fifteen days, none of Abu Zar's family members in Pakistan were notified about his whereabouts. 'The family was so upset; we were running everywhere, contacting police, airport authorities, and the airlines,' remembers Nazeer Ahmed, Abu Zar's brother in Pakistan. 'We couldn't find anything.' Eventually, after more searching, they learned that Abu Zar had successfully boarded his flight to Saudi Arabia, and even touched down on Saudi soil. Beyond that, details were scant.

In April 2012, seventeen days after his disappearance, relatives began pouring into the family home in Bhakkar district to offer condolences to the parents and siblings. Family members dissolved into elegiac verses. Most had resigned themselves to the idea that the worst had come to pass, convinced that Abu Zar had died a mysterious death. Even though there was no body to mourn, tears were shed.

Not long after the unforeseen funeral, however, Ahmed received a call from Saudi Arabia. To his astonishment, Abu Zar was still alive.

On the phone, Abu Zar said he had been booked on drug trafficking charges and sentenced to death by a Saudi court. He had tried to get in touch with Al-Sagheer, his Saudi employer, for any form of assistance, but the calls had gone unanswered. The family was dismayed to learn that Abu Zar's hearing took place without a lawyer, as the Saudi government held itself under no obligation to provide legal representation to the accused, including those facing the death penalty.

Following his arrest, Abu Zar was housed inside Briman jail in Jeddah, a multifunctional sand-coloured complex that served as a detention centre housing men, women and minors. During his initial stay, Abu Zar had lost contact with the outside world, and spent his days in detention listless and stressed. He told Nazeer Ahmed, his brother, that Briman jail provided decent enough food that he was still eating. But the mental anguish of detention often felt like a bullet piercing through him, he said.

Abu Zar feared death, and the time in jail allowed thoughts of little else, his brother said. Worse, Abu Zar did not know the exact day the execution would take place, only that it would transpire in some always-imminent future. The uncertainty weighed heavily on him, as it did for many prisoners who had no choice but to wait for their own execution. 'They don't tell a person beforehand,' said Ahmed. 'They just pick him from the prison and behead him.'

Abu Zar had appealed directly to the Pakistani and Saudi governments to be released, but his search for clemency bore no fruit. Meanwhile, Abu Zar was worried and anxious about how his children were faring in his absence. He had four children—two daughters and two sons—and he thought of them often while he was in prison. He furtively called his family back home in Pakistan by bribing a guard in the jail. Other prisoners kept phones illegally, bartering minutes on the phone among fellow inmates. The privilege of calling home was eagerly sought after by detainees.

'Prisoners have a right to see and meet their children,' his brother told me, saying that the family in Pakistan was not kept abreast of anything happening in Jeddah. Distressed by the lack of information, the family arranged an umrah [pilgrimage] visa for Abu Zar's father. 'He went to Saudi Arabia and submitted papers in the Pakistani embassy. He also met the judge.' Still, it changed little—Abu Zar remained in prison.

In recounting the situation, Abu Zar's brother lamented the Pakistani government's inattention and negligence. 'The people in the government didn't listen,' said Ahmed. 'They don't pay heed to his situation. What can we do about it?'

Indeed, for migrant workers detained on death row, the Saudi justice system often seems cruelly capricious. Sometimes detainees believe their punishment will span a fixed interval of time, only to realize the judges have arbitrarily modified the sentencing. 'They will give you a punishment of fifteen years imprisonment, and after five years they can change this and give you capital punishment,' Ahmed says. 'When a person is working in another country, he feels imprisoned even when he is free. So you can only imagine the condition of those who are actually in prisons there.'

Worse, the Saudi government rarely informs foreign embassies when a citizen is on death row, as required by the Vienna Convention on Consular Relations.[5] Many families never learn that their relatives are facing the gallows.

Ahmed adds that he's attempted to lodge complaints regarding the outcome of his brother's trial and detention several times, but there are few avenues open to report grievances.

*

Ahmed says that the worst moment is reserved for the time after the execution, not before: 'They don't send the body back to his family. They throw it away.' Sohail Yafat, an investigator with the JPP, echoes Ahmed's claim by saying that the Saudi criminal system does not give much hope to families who are looking for closure after capital punishment. Thanks to strict Islamic burial rites, the Saudi government often buries the dead bodies in unknown locations in the kingdom; families waiting to receive the bodies often wait interminably long intervals before being told that there was no body to send back. While this policy impacts migrant workers from a variety of countries, other foreign governments have been more active in addressing it. In 2017, neighbouring India had to petition the Saudi state for the repatriation of a woman's body to Kerala, India, a successful move that showed the impact of a government exerting pressure.[6] For Pakistani migrant workers, Islamabad's lack of diplomatic lobbying has meant that few, if any, deceased bodies are returned to the next of kin.

Theoretically, the mechanisms should already be in place to address these issues. Pakistani embassies and consulates across the globe employ 'community welfare attachés,' a department tasked with keeping track of any labour problems impacting Pakistani citizens in the destination country.[7] In addition to studying local labour market conditions (which, in the Gulf, often includes the abuse and exploitation of Pakistani labourers), the remit of the community welfare attaché also extends to taking note of how many Pakistani citizens are imprisoned in local jails and, in some cases, visiting them or notifying their families in Pakistan about the person's situation in jail. However, the majority of Pakistani prisoners in Saudi jails say that their embassy has never visited them in jail, according to the JPP. Pakistani diplomatic missions in Saudi

Arabia say they remain too chronically understaffed to review, let alone help address, the burgeoning prisoner population.

'Abu Zar's story is one case, but there are thousands of people in Saudi Arabia with the same story,' says Ahmed. His calls with Abu Zar allowed Ahmed to glean insight into how pervasive the detention of Pakistan drug traffickers was in the Saudi prison system. He says Pakistanis crowd the jails, and often have similar profiles: they fall prey to organized drug smuggling syndicates operating in Pakistan that lure migrant workers to the Gulf with promises of jobs that never materialize. Sometimes the migrants are asked to carry packages by a member of the group; other times, they are forced to ingest grammes of heroin at gunpoint. Often, they land on death row in Saudi Arabia, living in a state of limbo as the state decides when to mete out the punishment.

In the last few years, the number of Pakistanis have topped the list of foreigners executed on death row in Saudi Arabia.[8] While other South Asian countries have successfully exerted diplomatic pressure on Saudi Arabia to free their citizens (for example, asking Riyadh to commute a sentence or deport a worker), Pakistan has shied away from prodding its close ally to extend clemency or grant fairer or more lenient punishments proportionate to the severity of the crime. For example, the Philippines, one of the largest migrant-sending countries in Asia, not only takes up every case of a Filipino on death row in Saudi Arabia, it hires Saudi lawyers to defend its citizens.[9] Likewise, a Sri Lankan housemaid escaped death by stoning in 2015 after Colombo filed an appeal against the death sentence.[10] Overwhelmingly, when Riyadh has resolved death penalty cases without an execution, it has involved the foreign citizen's embassy or government directly entreating the Saudis to lift the punishment or commute the sentence.

Pakistan's Ministry of Foreign Affairs contends that it does not have bargaining power with Saudi Arabia to negotiate the release of its citizens. However, evidence suggests otherwise: given their historically robust military and political partnership, Pakistan would seem to enjoy qualitatively better relations with Saudi Arabia than other Asian states. As many as 70,000 Pakistani soldiers serve in Saudi Arabia's military, and Pakistan's former Chief of Army Staff, Raheel Sharif, was also tapped to lead Saudi Arabia's new counter-terrorism military alliance in January 2017. Moreover, beyond the US$2.5 billion in bilateral trade shared between the two Muslim countries, Pakistan's third-largest city, Faisalabad, is named in honour of the late Saudi King Faisal, whose name—and largesse—is also behind the construction of one of the largest mosques in Pakistan, the Faisal Mosque in Islamabad.

In 2014, when former Pakistani Prime Minister Nawaz Sharif visited Saudi Arabia, the late King Abdullah described the unwavering Pakistan-Saudi Arabia partnership in glowing terms, reiterating that Saudis would always support Pakistan's government and people.[11] Indeed, according to Crown Prince Mohammad bin Salman, Saudi Arabia has few allies like Pakistan: 'We consider Pakistan our second home,' he said.[12]

When Prime Minister Imran Khan visited Saudi Arabia in 2018 in search of economic assistance, he referenced the plight of migrant workers. 'I feel bad sometimes, because we have not been able to create the conditions that would keep them at home,' he told a Saudi audience.[20] 'All they do is work very hard here to feed their families.' In the lead-up to Khan's election, his party pledged to reform consular services for overseas Pakistanis. 'We will strengthen Pakistani embassies to provide emergency relief and other support to citizens facing hardship in case of any tragedy. We will provide consular and legal services to all Pakistanis jailed abroad,' claimed his party manifesto.[21] 'Our Ministry of Foreign Affairs must be focused on furthering not just Pakistan's interests abroad, but also ensuring protection of our citizens abroad.'

Indeed, without state-level intervention from Pakistan, families of migrants like Abu Zar have no choice but to accept that neither the Saudi nor the Pakistani government will stand with their family in their hour of need.

Notes

1. 'Indonesia halts execution of Pakistani drug convict,' *Express Tribune.* July 29, 2016 https://tribune.com.pk/story/1151537/indonesia-halts-execution-pakistani-drug-convict/

2. 'PM to take up Zulfiqar Ali's repatriation with Indonesian President: Asif.' SAMAA TV. January 25, 2018. https://www.samaa.tv/news/2018/01/pm-to-take-up-zulfiqar-alis-matter-with-indonesian-president-asif/

3. '"No Mercy" for Death Row Inmates.' *Jakarta Globe.* December 9, 2014. https://jakartaglobe.id/news/no-mercy-for-death-row-inmates/

4. 'CJ snubs govt over absence of policy on prisoners abroad,' *Dawn.* March 15, 2017. https://www.dawn.com/news/1320566

5. Vienna Convention on Consular Relations. 1963. http://legal.un.org/ilc/texts/instruments/english/conventions/9_2_1963.pdf

6. 'Saudi Arabia "spares" Sri Lankan maid in adultery case.' *BBC News.* December 23, 2015. https://www.bbc.com/news/world-asia-35166951.

7. Bureau of Emigration & Overseas Employment, https://beoe.gov.pk/community-welfare-attache-offices

8. A 2018 Human Rights Watch report says 'Saudi Arabia executes more Pakistanis than any other foreign nationality annually, nearly all for heroin smuggling, including 20 in 2014, 22 in 2015, 7 in 2016, and 17 in 2017' '"Caught in a Web:" Treatment of Pakistanis in the Saudi Criminal Justice System,' Human Rights Watch. March 7, 2018. https://www.hrw.org/report/2018/03/07/caught-web/treatment-pakistanis-saudi-criminal-justice-system

9. 'Saudi lawyers to help 8 Filipinos on death row.' March 22, 2018. PTV News. http://ptvnews.ph/saudi-lawyers-help-8-filipinos-death-row/

10. 'Saudi Arabia "spares" Sri Lankan maid in adultery case.' *BBC News.* December 23, 2015. https://www.bbc.com/news/world-asia-35166951

11. http://www.arabnews.com/news/featured/607811 Arab News. 2014.

12. Ibid.

13. As reported on Saudi news channels.

14. Full text of 2018 election manifesto available here: http://insaf.pk/public/insafpk/content/manifesto

People

The Gender Dynamics of Migration from Sri Lanka

In Sri Lanka, men still outstrip women when it comes to migrating for employment, but the balance is slowly changing. The numbers of women migrating are steadily picking up, despite a blitz of horrifying news about women workers returning from abroad maimed, or raped and pregnant, or even in coffins. According to the Government of Sri Lanka, these worst-case scenarios affect 4 per cent of Sri Lankan women labour migrants per year; however, the media spin is so pervasive that many people in Sri Lanka think that it is a given that ALL women migrants would be subjected to torture, rape or, more rarely, murder. This impression is equally pervasive among potential migrants getting ready to migrate for the first time. Why, then, would they be willing to go?

Poverty is the main impetus, a hard-hitting condition that leaves little alternative. The country is still recovering from a three decade-long civil war which has left much of its population desperate—particularly its rural, under-educated underprivileged masses. The poorest of the poor end up in the GCC countries, while those who have slightly better means, though remain desperate for jobs, pay to go to countries like Malaysia, Singapore and Hong Kong.

Latha's Story

Latha comes from a middle-class family in southern Sri Lanka. She finished high school and worked in Sri Lanka as a sales assistant, for which she was paid approximately US$100 a month. When her husband abandoned her with a young son, and her father passed away soon after, leaving her to support her mother and two school-going sisters as well, she found that her meagre income after ten years of working in Sri Lanka was not enough for everyone. She therefore opted to migrate for work, paying US$2,000 to a Colombo-based agent who promised her a receptionist's job at a well-known international hotel in Malaysia, with a salary of US$1,000 per month. Unfortunately for Latha, despite paying two years' worth of her Sri Lankan salary in 2014 to the agent for the promised new job, she ended up being trafficked.

She found herself working as a cleaner at the hotel instead of as a receptionist, and worse, boarded at a slum under extremely unhygienic conditions with other trafficked women. They were transported in private buses to and from work, with contact with outsiders kept to a minimum. She says she went unpaid, despite being promised that she would receive her pay eventually. When, after two months of this, she finally demanded to be paid and released, the management sent goons to beat her up over the next two months.

According to Migrant88 Malaysia, an aid agency working with such trafficked women, most likely it was not the well-known hotel itself exploiting her, as Latha believes. 'This was probably a case of a human trafficking syndicate subcontracting to valid employers. Most employers in Malaysia prefer to subcontract workers from agents, in order to overcome immigration bureaucracy. The many corruptions in our government system facilitate syndicates like these to thrive,' says Khadijah Shamsul, the program director of Migrant88.

Latha ended up running away to escape her enforced slavery, but then found herself in a very dangerous position on the streets of Malaysia as an undocumented worker. The Malaysian authorities crack down heavily on such workers, despite many of them having gone there legally and, like Latha, ending up 'undocumented' (i.e., with no valid work permit or passport) due to no fault of their own. Latha's passport had remained with her traffickers when she ran away. After a few months on the streets, she fell into the hands of sex traffickers. She was offered a home by a Malaysian woman, whom she thought meant well, but the woman sold her into sexual slavery, pretending to Latha that she would be employed as a domestic worker. Several months later, she ran away again, and was then rescued by Migrant88 and placed in a legitimate cleaner's job, with a monthly salary of US$500. Altogether, she spent more than one and a half years being trafficked or on the streets, before she got a stable, secure job.

However, in 2017, the two-year limit for her work permit was coming to an end and she needed to renew it. To do this, agents again demanded US$2,000. The bureaucratic system in Malaysia is such that, despite having a corporate employer willing to employ her, neither the employer nor Latha could access the work permit directly. The red tape in place ensures that both parties must go through agents with inside contacts at the relevant ministries to access work permits.

Yet, when I met her in Malaysia via the aid agency that had rescued her, Latha, then thirty-three years old, said that she would go back to Sri Lanka to renew her permit, to return to Malaysia as a documented worker. She would again have to pay US$2,000, to get back to a cleaning job that pays her US$500.

Why did she think it would be worth it? Within her two short years in Malaysia, she had suffered an extreme range of physical, emotional and sexual violence.

'There are no jobs in Sri Lanka for people like me,' she answered. 'Especially jobs that will pay at rates enabling our families to survive. I will take a loan in Sri Lanka, come back here, and continue to earn. There is no alternative.'

I asked her whether she still thought it was better to pay to return to Malaysia, as opposed to getting a cash gift worth the same amount to work in the Gulf instead. 'Yes,' was her emphatic answer. 'Too many domestic workers' coffins return from the Gulf. I am better off in Malaysia.'

In short, despite ending up trafficked and in slavery in Malaysia;

after being repeatedly abused by police as an undocumented worker when she escaped; after getting picked up by a sex trafficking ring and escaping them too, Latha thought it was worthwhile to pay four months of her current Malaysian salary to be able to return to Malaysia—and that her own experiences were still better than those faced by her counterparts in the Gulf countries.

*

In the GCC countries, conditions are indeed terrible for migrant workers; though that is not to say that Malaysia is much better. However, after the negative media portrayal of the hazards faced by women working in the Gulf in the early 2000s, many Sri Lankan women were scared away from migrating there. Now, those countries offer Sri Lankan women a cash incentive to beckon them—and it works. Far more Sri Lankan women end up in the Gulf than in Malaysia or Singapore, because while women have to pay hefty agents' fees to get to the two South Asian countries, they are given a cash gift of US$1,500 if they decide to migrate to the GCC countries as domestic workers.

Many households are now in severe debt in Sri Lanka, and such cash incentives impel women, who would not otherwise consider migrating to the GCC countries, to go. Many are indeed forced to go by their husbands or parents. This development is directly at variance with the local heavily patriarchal culture, in which men consider themselves the sole breadwinners and expect women to be confined to the home and hearth. Yet, in the current migration stakes, men would have to pay US$1,500–2,000 in agents' fees to get to the Gulf, while women are gifted the same amount in cash to go instead.

A Society at Odds with Itself

This situation has given rise to a society at odds with itself, in which women are compelled to be the breadwinners, yet are castigated for it. In villages where women migrate in significant numbers, charges abound that the women:

- Would be sexually licentious once set 'free' in those foreign countries. They need the familial, cultural and social restrictions of the village to keep them in check apparently.
- Would come back with sexually-transmitted diseases and therefore be sickly, because almost certainly they would have been raped by their employer—which is somehow considered their fault as well. Not much sympathy is exhibited for the women.
- That they are terrible mothers to their children for leaving them in the care of the fathers or guardians. Childcare is seen as solely the mother's duty, and it is assumed that that should be her primary responsibility.
- That they would be too 'independent' by the time they return, having become 'arrogant' by working abroad. And by that it is meant that the women would no longer be meek and subservient and content to remain at home.

All these charges are laid against women who are about to migrate, have migrated, or have returned.

Komala Devi's Story

Komala Devi (name changed) is forty-six. She is currently in Saudi Arabia, though not in direct contact with her family in Sri Lanka. She indicated that she might be in abusive employment in a letter home some years ago. Her three children are being looked after by her seventy-seven-year-old mother-in-law, who roasts and sells peanuts for a living.

In the words of her mother-in-law: 'My daughter in law was naïve. She borrowed a gold necklace and bangles for a friend to wear to a wedding, from another friend of hers. The woman she gave the jewellery to, pawned it off instead. My daughter-in-law was caught in the middle between two families threatening her: those who gave the jewellery, as well as those who took it.

'It caused a scandal in our neighbourhood which affected us all. My daughter-in-law was ostracized as a cheat, with both families spreading rumours about her. She went to the family she had given the jewellery to, begging for it back, and got beaten up by them. Unable to bear the humiliation, she ran away.

'My son was a fisherman. He couldn't bear the rumours of his wife being an unchaste woman as well as a cheat who had abandoned her family, and he committed suicide. I am looking after my three grandchildren now. All I want is my daughter-in-law to come back so that I can die in peace.

'She sent a letter some years ago, saying she was in Saudi Arabia without access to a phone and working under very difficult conditions, without regular pay. She said she needed to earn to pay off that lost jewellery and would not return until then.'

Meanwhile, the men left behind are rarely productive at home. Many just drink away the remittances, thus ensuring that all the abuse that women go through as domestic workers in the GCC countries to send over meagre remittances of US$150–200, is for naught.

Subadra Nafiz's Story

Subadra has worked twice in Saudi Arabia, returned for a year, and is now heading out to Kuwait again at the age of thirty-four. 'I left when I was seventeen the first time,' she says. 'I had to work hard round the clock, looking after an extended family in a house spanning five storeys, and managed to sleep only two hours a day.

'Other than the hard work and the lack of sleep, there was no problem with the employment. I sent all the money I earned to my mother, but she used it all up, so I had no savings when I returned. She's my adopted mother with other children of her own, I am a war orphan.

'Then I got married, and my husband didn't have a regular income either, so I left again for Saudi Arabia. He used my remittances to drink, and married another woman without telling me. Thus again, I returned home to nothing. I have to go back to earn.'

Subadra lived in the former war zone of Vavuniya, a rural area without many prospects for employment, other than through predatory leasing companies that sell high-value goods like TVs and stereo equipment on installment and take them away when the villagers are unable to pay, driving a war-affected people further into debt. She explained why she is resigned to returning to the Gulf. 'There are no opportunities for women to earn here. I have stayed and tried insurance, leasing, marketing—those are the office jobs available here and I tried them all. They pay exploitative rates and our take-home pay is cut often. Despite the exploitation abroad, at least I will manage to save something.'

A minority of men do engage in productive work back home, or at the very least ensure that their wife's remittances are gainfully used. In the majority of cases however, the women come back to find that the husband has become an abusive alcoholic. Often, the children have been subjected to various forms of physical, emotional and even sexual abuse, if not by the father, then by others who know how to target a drunk father's vulnerable children, with the result that the children end up being school dropouts too. Worse, many women are beaten by their husbands as a way of forcing them to return to the Gulf, so that he can continue his lifestyle. The lack of support from home also makes them even more vulnerable to exploitation abroad.

Vidhya Gangatharan's Story

'I slept only two hours [a night] for five years in Saudi Arabia. The employers were very nice otherwise. They didn't pay me until I returned however, and gave my money as a lump sum for the five years' service. I was happy with the amount until I reached home and an educated relative did the maths and told me I had been cheated of three years' worth of salary. I am illiterate and so didn't realize the numbers didn't add up,' says Vidhya, who fled domestic abuse at home. She had been happy to agree to the employers' proposal that they pay her a lump sum when she returned, as she had fled an alcoholic husband back home whom she feared would drink away her remittances.

Life in Sri Lanka: Laws and Culture Both Constrain Women

A question that crops up repeatedly when women seek to migrate is who controls the use of their bodies?

Sri Lanka has state laws ensuring basic human rights enshrined in the constitution, yet archaic community and/or religious laws still take precedence over them, even according to the constitution. Unsurprisingly, most such community/religious laws are heavily discriminatory against women. As in India, Muslim women in Sri Lanka have particularly been fighting to do away with the discriminatory community laws pertaining to them. They are pitted against the men in their community however, who demand the laws never be changed, citing religious sentiment, with the state spinelessly deciding to not take action on the matter until the community resolves it from within; an impasse since 50 per cent of the community are pitted against the other half. Women from other communities often have problems with their own community laws too, such as the Thesavalamai law followed in Jaffna, which is discriminatory to Tamil women. A woman can do little under this law without her husband's signature. Yet campaigns to make the law equal for everybody have thus far made little progress in Sri Lanka.

Educated women in cities are better off than rural women, as they have access to formal employment to some extent. In the rural areas, from where most of the migrant women are drawn however, farming, fishing and toddy tapping are the main industries; and community, religious and cultural rules prevent them from engaging in paid work. The few women who break the rules to engage in such work are ostracized. While women do own land and farm to some extent, they are often kept out of the farming societies by men, so that they cannot directly access the benefits, trainings and grants given by aid agencies and the government. They are not allowed to engage in fishing and toddy tapping at all by their husbands, fathers and brothers. At best, they can take part in post-production work at home, for which they are usually not paid.

When these husbands, fathers or brothers have either died or gone missing in war, or else descended into substance abuse after the war, such women have little alternative other than to seek work as domestic workers abroad.

Nalaini Kandasamy's Story

Nalaini first went to Saudi Arabia as a sixteen-year-old in 2005. Most of her family had escaped the war to refugee camps in India, but her mother, she, and a younger brother stayed in Sri Lanka as the brother was unwell. They lived in Vavuniya, where the LTTE used to conscript one child per family for their forces. Nalaini was the one targeted, as her younger brother was too sickly.

Her mother got an agent to forge documents increasing Nalaini's age to adulthood, and sent her to Saudi Arabia. She worked for some years there, then fell in love with an Indian restaurant worker, got pregnant and had to return to Sri Lanka.

Now twenty-eight, she says it has been a hard few years trying to survive, as she couldn't get a stable job in Sri Lanka. The last job she applied for in Sri Lanka was at a garment factory where she was told she looked overweight and thus unlikely to be fit enough to stand at the sewing machines for eight hours or more a day.

As per Sri Lankan government regulations, since 2007, women cannot migrate out of the country if any of their children are under five years of age. Nalaini's daughter is older than five now, so she plans to leave her in the care of her mother and take up employment in the Gulf again.

'There are far more regulations pertaining to women than for men, when it comes to migrating abroad for work', said Vavuniya Assistant Divisional Secretary, Sarathanjali Manoharan. 'As per government regulations, women going abroad for work should:

- Obtain a certification of residence as well as a character certificate from their respective Government village officers.;
- Register a form outlining the condition of their house: whether it has toilets, doors, windows (for the safety of the children left behind), which should be signed by their husbands or the guardians in whose care they leave their children;

- Submit to multiple home visits and reports on the situation of the children and family back home, by government field officers, including development officers, women development officers, child-rights promotion officers, early childhood rights promotion officers and midwives.'

None of these rules apply to the men. The onus of childcare, and making alternative arrangements for childcare, is primarily on the women, not only in society's view but also enforced by the government's rules and attempts at regulating migration.

Sexual Abuse of Aspiring Migrants in Sri Lanka

Due to lack of information, many women are led to believe that they owe agents sexual favours before they can migrate. Many are so desperate to leave that they give in.

A common problem arising from this practice is that some women would arrive pregnant at the destination country. To resolve this, the agents have come up with measures of their own. They coercively inject the women with Depo-Provera, an injection that is supposed to act as a three-month contraceptive, but has been widely banned in many countries due to its horrific side-effects, including massive loss of bone density. In many cases, the women are not even told that they are being given the injections, but they report the side-effects of the injections soon after medical checkups arranged by the agents—dizziness, nausea, boils all over the body, weakness and tiredness.

While the government once acknowledged that such injections were being given, and took steps due to activists' outrage to outlaw it, this simply made the practice go underground. The result is that there is no official acknowledgement about what is happening to the women's bodies now, not even to the women themselves.

According to Rahini Baskaran, a community worker in Eastern Sri Lanka, agents actively solicit certain categories of vulnerable women for migration, in order to sexually exploit them as well as live off their earnings. The long drawn out war has left a number of women in such categories behind, including widows, single or divorced women, wives of disabled men, or men who are otherwise unable to be the main breadwinner, and wives of men who have migrated abroad for work. According to Baskaran, apart from the above, they also target struggling mothers with many children, and women in households that have gone heavily into debt due to badly managed microfinance loans. A lot of women are thus vulnerable, in post-war Sri Lanka.

While many women are more aware now, thanks to activists' outreach, they often remain helpless. When the forces around their home circumstances impel them to leave, they do not feel they have a choice about saying no to contraceptive injections, saying no to agents who try to sexually solicit them, or saying no to exploitative work conditions in the destination countries.

Women's Experiences in GCC Countries

Perhaps unsurprisingly, when speaking to migrant returnees in Sri Lanka, one often finds that the women do not regret going to work in the GCC countries.

Many of them outline the horrific conditions in which they had worked—having to sleep on the bare floor of a hot storeroom, working twenty-two-hour days with barely two hours of sleep, working without rest for several families in an extended family unit—yet they maintain they have been lucky. As they had migrated fearing the spectres of torture, rape and murder that they regularly see reported in local media, they feel that if *all* they had to contend with were the long hours, lack of sleep and exceptionally hard work, they have been 'lucky'.

As they pointed out, some of the conditions, such as the long hours of unremitting domestic work, are not very different from their own homes in Sri Lanka. They might get a few more hours of sleep back home, but from dawn to midnight, they would be engaged in similar labour. The only difference is that in the GCC countries, they are being paid for that labour. Yes, it is abysmal pay—but for the gender that has religious, social and cultural norms preventing it from taking part in paid labour back home, work in the Gulf can be an improvement.

Indeed, as noted by their village critics, many of the women who go abroad come back 'independent minded'—they are no longer subservient, content to be meek or quiet. What empowers them in the Gulf? The very fact of becoming a breadwinner for the whole family is one reason, but there are others too.

'I loved the freedom in Saudi Arabia to evaluate and understand myself as a person. Over here, we face a constant barrage of criticism from society, friends and family to be a certain way. It was while there, removed from our society's constant harsh feedback on who I was supposed to be and how I was supposed to stay within those rigidly set boundaries, that I managed to evaluate myself and came to understand my own thoughts, needs and personality. I discovered myself while out there,' says Stella, a forty-seven-year-old returnee in North Sri Lanka.

In answer to a follow-up question about what kind of freedoms she'd had in Saudi Arabia to explore and discover herself, she replied, 'Oh, I didn't mean freedom in terms of time, or ability to go out anywhere or do anything other than housework. I worked round the clock, other than for the six hours I slept. They were exceptionally nice employers, you know? They allowed me six hours of sleep, unlike most other employers there.

'The only time I went out was once a week to do shopping. I had to cover myself in a black abaya and the lady of the house would come with me in the car, driven either by her husband or driver, to supervise my shopping. No, I meant freedom to process my own thoughts and understand myself contextually, in the absence of the barrage of constant criticism that gets thrown at us women here, as to who we should be and how we should behave, with little regard to our own thoughts and feelings on the matter.

'It was good for me to remove myself from our culture for a while and be placed in a completely foreign culture, so that I could evaluate our society from a distance and come to my own conclusions on how I would reintegrate into it, once I came back.'

Another woman exemplified what changed for her, with an anecdote: 'Over here, we do all the domestic chores, scorned as "women's work," and are often unthanked and unpaid for it. Over there, my employers were grateful for the work I was doing for them, even though they were paying me for it. It served as a massive boost to my self-esteem. I went from feeling worthless and a burden on society to the realization that the work I do, whether unpaid or not, is valuable too.

'Back home, we women would cook the food, and then be the last to eat it. One day, at my employer's house, I saw some cut fruits left behind on the dining table, and decided to eat them, as per years of ingrained habit of not letting anything go to waste.

'That was one of the few times my employer ever spoke sharply to me. She told me that I was never to eat their leftovers again, to take whatever I wanted fresh from the kitchen, and if I didn't have food according to my fancy already stocked there, to let her know and she would stock it for me. It was the first time I realized I was entitled to fresh, new food on my own. I wasn't obliged to wait for others to eat before finishing what was left.'

And that is the attitude she has come back with: that she is a person with basic rights to dignity in her own right, that the 'women's work' she does is valuable too—at direct variance with what society tells her. How does she cope now in Sri Lanka?

'People will always wag their tongues. I just don't listen. They are like frogs in the well. At least I got to jump out of the well, if only briefly, to get a glimpse of the outside world. I value that experience, and pay no heed to a society that says I was tainted by the experience.'

Yet are the working conditions that women like these two, and many more, found empowering really that empowering? Both the above women had to work from dawn till late into the night without rest. Others recount that they often didn't finish their work until well after midnight, yet had to be up well before dawn to tend to multiple families' needs before the children went to school and the adults to work. Many more have visibly-puffed, red eyes even to this day.

There was no concept of ever being able to take a break in between, nor any off days or holidays other than a two-week break every two years. It is common to hear descriptions like:

'We could never use any of the chairs in those homes. If we sat down on the floor for even a few minutes, the women of the house would scold us for slacking.'

Or:

'The employment was good but we only had two to three hours of sleep per day.'

As is evident from the above quotes, many women have a skewed perception and a very low threshold for what they termed 'good employment'. It is a testament to how bad things are in Sri Lanka that women who have worked or are continuing to work in the Gulf find the conditions there 'empowering.'

Sexual Abuse in the GCC

Most returnees were reluctant to talk about any sexual abuse they might have faced, understandably, in the context of the stigma they face over it in their communities. As such, many took pains to say that their male employers had never even talked to or interacted with them. In the words of one returnee: 'People here claim that we must be sick with sexually-transmitted diseases because we returned from the Middle East. How dare they? When it comes to culture, do they know how much more cultured the Gulf countries are? I was in Kuwait for seven years. The maama [lady of the house] would regularly check my phone every week to see if I had any other numbers or unwarranted phone call activity. I was allowed to have only her number and my Sri Lankan family's number on my phone—and phone calls would be tolerated only to those two numbers. We were never allowed to go out of the house unless they took us somewhere. How could we be anything other than scrupulously moral in such a setting?

'As for clothes, we had to be covered head to toe in black, even in the house. Only my face would show. The men of the house would not even talk to or look at us. They would communicate whatever they needed from us through the lady of the house. We lived in a far more cultured place than anyone here, and yet they dare call us sexually corrupted when we return.'

In her view then, the more culturally strict the destination country, the more moral it was for women like herself to migrate to.

In a few cases however, after first denying they had been abused, some became comfortable enough over the interview period to detail stories of active sexual abuse. Though none admitted to rape, they did admit to being groped and to receiving unwanted sexual solicitations, though always with the entreaty, 'Please do not publish these details under our names. We face enough stigma over here already.' Having endured sexual abuse of varying levels, they see little alternative other than to silently bear it and to cover it up, whilst cringing at the many aspersions cast on their character and reputation back home.

Rani Sinnathamby's Story

Rani Sinnathamby (name changed) had worked in Saudi Arabia twice over the previous four years, and was scheduled to leave for Kuwait again at the age of forty-five, when I met her. Of her four children, two died or disappeared in the war, which she is still traumatized by.

'My elder son died in a LTTE claymore attack in 2006, and my younger son disappeared after being arrested for it thirty days later,' she recounts. 'After the claymore attack in which my elder son and three other villagers died, the Army surrounded our village and got down a thalayatti [an informant who wears a hood and indicates potential LTTE cadres with a nod of his head]. My second son, aged seventeen, had just returned from his A-level exams. We were still in shock about the elder son's death, soon after which my mother died of grief too. The thalayatti, among all the young men grouped before him, nodded at my younger son. The Army soldiers dragged him away in a truck, kicking and screaming. At the Army camp, when we went after him, they denied taking him. I have been running from pillar to post trying to find him ever since.' She broke down crying as she recalled this.

Her husband, a carpenter, descended into alcoholism after the loss of his sons, so she had to go abroad to Saudi Arabia to be the breadwinner for the family. In Saudi Arabia, she was sexually harassed by her employer often, but she had no-one she could talk to about it. She once called a nephew of her husband's working in Riyadh for help. He told her not to let his uncle know about what she was going through, but also told her not to give up her job as her remittance was needed back home.

Back in Sri Lanka now, she is highly defensive about other people casting aspersions on her character for having been the victim of sexual abuse. Villagers heap scorn on migrant returnees such as herself, calling them sexually corrupted due to the abuse they are assumed to have undergone, so she takes care to 'put them right' on how very well and respectfully she was treated by her employers. She told us the same thing too, before unwinding over the course of a long interview—then like many others before her, requested that she not be shamed by having her name and picture published along with the details of her sexual abuse.

This is a matter that crops up like clockwork. Women who have been sexually abused have no recourse open to them to heal. When they are stigmatized, instead of being offered sympathy for the abuse they have undergone, they have little choice but to stoically deny that they have been abused at all.

Conclusion

Every year, during International Women's Day celebrations in Sri Lanka, women's contribution to the country is highly lauded. Migrant women are the highest source of foreign exchange to the country. Their remittances form the backbone of the Sri Lankan economy, which is acknowledged repeatedly. Yet, while the country grows rich off their labour, they remain poor. And, at an individual level, their rights are continually violated—by their families, by their communities, by the Sri Lankan state and by their employers in the destination countries. Their combined power is acknowledged; their individual rights are denied.

Conflict, Poverty and Climate Change Drive Sri Lankans to Migrate

AMANTHA PERERA

Climate Change

Adigama, Sri Lanka, once used to be picturesque. It would be still, if the sun did not glare down, causing temperatures to soar above 34°C every other day. In late 2017, this small village in Puttalam District, 170 kilometres north-west of the capital, Colombo, is parched and barren, resembling something from a grim movie rather than an agricultural settlement. The large reservoir nearby looks like a massive arid plain, and the boats that used to travel to the middle of the lake to fish are marooned at the edge of the little water that remains.

Sisira Kumara is the main administrative officer in this village. He works out of a one-room office that shares the compound of a government-run preschool. Dressed immaculately in white shirt and black trousers, he gives a wry smile when I ask him about the impact of the drought, a question he has become sick of answering during the last year.

'Look around, do you see any young men? That is the impact,' he says with a hint of a smile.

But there is a young man walking past his office and I almost scream: 'There!'

He looks up and nonchalantly deadpans, 'He is visiting here while on leave.'

What Kumara is trying to explain is that with rains and droughts destroying the harvests since 2016, young men and women from his village are leaving—in hordes. There are 416 families in the village, which has an estimated population of about 2,500. He suspects that between 200 to 250 youth have fled the village. 'We have never seen this kind of an exodus ever,' says Kumara, who himself is not that old at twenty-seven.

The problem is that this village has been dependent on agriculture, specifically the cultivation of paddy and vegetables, for income. Kumara assesses that more than 70 per cent of the village income traditionally used to come from agriculture. The farms are completely dependent on rain for water. Generation after generation in villages like Adigama have grown accustomed to heavy rains from May into July, leading into the main harvest, followed by drier months till October and November, and then minor rains between November and January, which provide for the secondary planting season. That age-old pattern has been disrupted like never before during the past decade. The rains have played havoc, destroying the harvests which are lastingly tied to the monsoon cycle. For example, between July 2016 and end April 2018, there were no significant rains, and consequently, no money to be made from agriculture. Then, over 350 mm of rain fell during a single week at the end of May 2018, the highest rainfall recorded in the area for at least two decades. Households for whom the nearest clean water usually lay a one-hour trek away, past dried-out reservoirs, suddenly found themselves submerged in ten-foot-high flood waters.

Harvests were traditionally sold in raw form to outsiders, and all value addition took place away from the village. There still aren't many jobs beyond those few required for cultivation. There are no banking or other financial institutions in the village, other than the local money-lenders. The nearest bank is 20 kilometres away, a three-hour journey by bus on a good day. There is no infrastructure in this village to speak of, apart from the power lines, the pothole-infested roads and old farm tools.

Kumara says that it is no big surprise that those his age and younger are trying their luck elsewhere and wanting to follow a much-trodden path to riches. Youth who view working on their ancestral paddy lands as heavy, unsavoury labour will seek jobs in Colombo or its suburbs. 'There is no money in agriculture; it is back-breaking work and people don't see farmers becoming millionaires or owning nice cars, so they want to follow those who have done that,' Kumara says.

The easiest jobs to get are as office helpers or as manual labour at the many construction sites in Colombo. But many hope and plan for such jobs as just the start of a more productive, longer journey. Kumara says that the ultimate aim is to go overseas—to the Middle East, East Asia or even Europe.

In 2017, of the 212,000 Sri Lankans who left the island as migrant labour, 106,000 were men, 65,000 of whom were skilled labourers while 51,000 were unskilled. Specialized research showing that at least some of these migrants were moving because of climate extremes does not exist in Sri Lanka, but anecdotal evidence from villages like Adigama show that there is at least a pattern of increasing migration due to harvest failures.

Government officials say that this kind of migration out of agricultural areas is now a common phenomenon. 'Farmers are moving out of their villages because there is no money in agriculture,' says M.W. Weerakoon, an additional secretary at the Ministry of Agriculture. He calculates that a rice farmer needs to plant at least an acre of paddy and make sure that there are no harvest losses to be able to make at least US$115 per month—just enough to keep a family of four above the poverty line. A maize farmer would need about 50 per cent more land to make the same amount of money.

'No one, no small farmer I know of, is making that kind of money,' Weerakoon says. To add to their woes, land ownership by individual farmers has been on the slide and, on average, a Sri Lankan paddy farmer owns and cultivates less than an acre.

'So, what do these farmers or their children do? They seek jobs that pay well,' Weerakoon says, adding, 'even if that means working in a foreign country with little or no rights and freedoms. Most would take that as a bargain, given the money they make.'

Bilesha Weeraratne, a researcher with the Institute of Policy Studies, a Colombo-based policy agency, says that due to erratic weather patterns, 'large numbers are moving due to climate risks [and] families feel safer when a member is outside the zone of climate risk.' Essentially, families dependent on agriculture now feel safer when they have more income options—which means members must work outside the traditional agro-based economy.

Districts like Puttalam are particularly vulnerable to such migration because of the lack of jobs and the dependency on agriculture. The World Food Programme and the UN Food and Agriculture Organisation found that the 2017 drought, which they assessed as the worst in forty years, had continued into the first quarter of 2018 in Puttalam. 'It will impact once again, like last year, the availability of drinking water, food prices and agricultural labour opportunities,' a joint disaster assessment released in April 2018, said.[1] Ironically, the drought cycle was broken in 2018, but by floods, which continued to make agriculture an unviable option for the residents. And, by the third quarter of 2018, another drought was plaguing the region again.

*

W.M. Suranga, a twenty-three-year-old has already started his journey away from Adigama. After witnessing his family paddy plot undergo one harvest failure after another, he decided to shift to Colombo.

Now, he sends some money home when he can, and his parents can survive without the added pressure of another mouth to feed. When Suranga was small, things were different. His father would make enough money from their two-acre plot and the family never felt that it was in danger of getting into debt. In fact, Suranga felt that his was one of the more affluent families in the neighbourhood. There was the occasional harvest failure, but nothing like what they have witnessed in the last five years. As their losses mounted, his father was forced into debt. 'There was really no option; we were on the verge of selling our lands when I decided to leave,' explains Suranga.

Nightmare in the Gulf

'I moved to Colombo and first worked at a construction site. Now I work as the office assistant in the same firm. I get a guaranteed pay and if I can work a bit longer I can go to the Gulf,' Suranga says. He earns around US$250 a month and can save around US$100 if he tries hard. 'In the Gulf you can get three, four times that money.'

Despite the money, working overseas as a migrant worker is no easy task. Suranga knows all about these horror stories. He has friends from his village and from his Colombo crowd that have gone to the GCC countries as workers. 'It will be hard, harder than anything I have ever done, but the money is good,' he says.

The hardships experienced by male migrant workers are not that well known in Sri Lanka. But those who have gone to work in countries like the United Arab Emirates, Qatar and Bahrain, talk of virtual slave labour and chain-gangs working on large sites. Suranga says that his friends, especially those working on construction sites or as unskilled labourers, talk of the dire conditions: quarters which are nothing more than wooden shacks; long working hours, six days a week; no medical care or other benefits.

'There is also the fear of rape. It's all men in those compounds and no women. There is lots of talk of young men being raped or being forced into relationships with other men. Because of our culture, we don't talk about these things, but that is the truth,' Suranga says.

The Sri Lanka Foreign Employment Bureau does not even have a category for complaints about abuse. Suranga's description of the suffering is all second-hand. It took me several phone calls to get him to put me in touch with someone who had undergone it himself.

*

Ajith* shared the same dreams as Suranga: escaping poverty and, in his own words, 'becoming a millionaire'. In 2011, he left for Qatar to work as a construction worker. He had already worked on construction sites in Sri Lanka as a supervisor, but the lack

---

*Name changed at his request

of formal training meant that he had to take a lower-status job. He took it because of the pay it promised—at US$350, it was still higher than what he was earning in Sri Lanka. But he was thrilled that two years after leaving his rural village in Polonnaruwa District (another region dependent on agriculture about 300 kilometres from Colombo), he was finally on a plane, following his dreams.

He did not worry too much about the fact that he'd had to borrow US$1,700 to pay the agents to secure the job. Once he landed in Qatar, officials from the company took his passport, informing him that they had paid the agents to secure his services and he could not leave for at least eighteen months. That was the first of a series of rude surprises.

He had to live with twenty other Sri Lankans and Indians in a small shack. There was no warm welcome, just a shove that directed him to the dingiest corner of the shack, the accepted place for any newcomer. His salary was half of the amount that he had been promised and he had to pay for food in an alien country. At work, which started the day after his arrival, he found that his job included everything from carrying buckets of cement to balancing dozens of tea cups at once.

The pecking orders at his work site and his lodgings were overbearing. For example, he had to wait in line and be the last to use the toilets in the mornings. 'So I tried getting up very early, but then it was too cold, I was too tired and was afraid to wake up others while walking to the toilet,' he recalls. He was constantly homesick. To make matters even worse, when he adamantly rejected sexual advances by other men, he was ostracized. 'It was crazy; it was all work, more work, little food, heat, and men trying to have sex with me. It was not a good situation.' The desert climate also was not to his liking, he said, adding that the dust, sun and the heat were intolerable. When he fell sick, he was asked to continue working or risk losing pay for the absent days.

Ajith, however, kept his woes to himself. In phone calls back home, he pretended everything was fine. His wife could sense that something was amiss, but Ajith brushed it aside, saying that he was too tired from the hard work. 'I started keeping a calendar like a small boy marking out holidays, counting down to the day when I could get out of the camp.'

But he felt his suffering was paying off. Finally, after about a year, he began sending money back home and his wife started building a small house in his village. Around the same time, he moved to another area where he had far more accommodating colleagues. His living conditions improved a bit—no longer was he last in line for the bathrooms—but his work conditions remained abysmal. There was no over-time, no sick leave and, even a year after joining the firm, he was still carrying cement buckets and tea cups.

After eighteen months, he got his passport back and returned home for a break. 'When I saw my small house under construction, all those days of suffering meant nothing.'

He once again approached manpower agencies for a job in the GCC. This time, however, he knew the ropes well enough to avoid financially crippling contract clauses. With the help of a professional translator, he got the draft contract translated and also made sure that it was legally binding. He was finally able to secure a job as a supervisor, after a search of six months.

Ajith says that government authorities should do more to build awareness about the work conditions, lodging and culture shocks that migrant workers face. 'When I went abroad, I paid the fees to the Foreign Employment Bureau, but no one told me what I was getting into, what kind of life I was heading to,' he says. He also thinks they should set up a mechanism whereby job contracts can be translated.

Ajith is critical of Sri Lanka's overseas missions in the GCC, arguing that they are only keen to avoid diplomatic or political incidents. 'They just want to make sure that Sri Lankan workers can get into those countries, so they work with the job agents to make sure that happens. They are also so under-staffed that they cannot effectively look after a large workforce.'

Vultures in the Middle

The most influential players in this world, according to Ajith are the manpower agencies and job agents. They use touts to scour remote villages and approach potential workers, sometimes with disastrous consequences. The worst such case is of twenty-four-year-old Rizana Nafeek, a young Sri Lankan woman from the remote Trincomalee District, who was beheaded in Saudi Arabia for infanticide in 2013. Nafeek had already spent eight years in jail in Saudi Arabia, first charged with murder and then on death row. All government and private efforts to seek a pardon for her failed. She was executed unannounced when the victim's family denied her clemency.

Nafeek went to Saudi Arabia when she was seventeen years old, well below the legal age for foreign employment, using a forged passport. Her family members told me that they were approached by a person from a nearby village, who promised them that their daughter would earn well in the Middle East. Later, they found out that the person was an agent for a recruitment agency in Colombo, and got a commission for every successful recruit. The family's main income came from collecting firewood in the nearby forests. That, however, was a risky task during the Sri Lankan civil conflict, with both government troops and insurgents using the jungles as cover for attacks. The main reason why Rizana went overseas was poverty and the lack of options for breaking out of it. 'Because we were poor and without any real way to make money, they manipulated the situation,' Rizana's mother, Razeena, told me.

When Rizana was first detained, her family was shocked but thought they could secure her release. Razeena fought for eight years to get her daughter released.

Just before Rizana was executed, I met her at her half-built house. It's not the easiest job in the world to ask a suffering person the same questions that have been asked a hundred times before; it's even worse when those questions are along the lines of: 'How do you feel about your daughter being on death row in a prison in Saudi Arabia? Do you think she will be pardoned?' It made me feel like a vulture circling someone about to die. But I had to ask them.

Razeena was dignified. She did not cry for the camera. Her answers were that of a mother trying to save her daughter from a terrible death. 'I want my daughter back,' she told me as I held the sugar-laden tea she had served me. Soon after our meeting, she got to meet Rizana one last time, but she never got her daughter back. With the media hype about the execution over, now the name Rizana Nafeek is just another footnote, rarely mentioned.

Since the execution, two successive Sri Lankan governments have tried to rein in the recruitment agencies, but loose labour laws in destination countries still allow for some terrible situations.

Ajith says that hundreds of Sri Lankans arrive in the Gulf every year without even having read their agreements. 'Some don't even know how to read the details of their own passport. While travelling on the Gulf route, I have filled embarkation papers for migrant workers on dozens of occasions.' The workers who seek such help are those who either cannot read, or who are unable to understand the simple instructions given in three languages.

Worryingly, the bulk of these leave Sri Lanka legitimately, most of them armed with Foreign Employment Bureau certificates that attest that they have undergone training. Domestic workers who travel to the Middle East now have to pay 10,000 Sri Lankan rupees (US$57) and undergo a three-week training course with the Bureau. The training provides everything from basic language skills and experience with electronic appliances to advice and some cultural tips. That training itself has been questioned by many.

Several months before Rizana Nafeek was executed, another Sri Lankan woman, Lahandapurege Ariyawathie, landed in Saudi Arabia with the Bureau's certificate in hand and a dream of owning a house of her own. Although much older than Nafeek at fifty-four years, she, too, aimed to be a domestic worker in a Saudi household. What she did not know was that she was headed to a house almost 100 kilometres away from any city. She was going to be a domestic worker in a household that was almost as poor as her own family. She only worked there for five months and returned home with oozing wounds and a body that looked like it had been crucified.

Ariyawathie says that the training she got was not sufficient. Her troubles began when she burnt an electric appliance. In her defence, she says that the blender was completely different from the type she was trained on in Sri Lanka, and she could not learn the instructions. 'I could not communicate, I only learnt how to say "hello", "how are you", that kind of thing during my training, I could not explain that I was having trouble using the appliances.'

As the days wore on, the frustration mounted in the household. Ariyawathie also realized that she was a status symbol—finally the family had become rich enough to afford a foreign maid. But with the maid in question becoming a liability rather than a badge of riches, they soon began physically abusing her. Ariyawathie told me that while the wife held her down, the husband would burn her with heated nails that he inserted into her arms and legs.

Once her wounds became infested and began smelling, they abandoned her at a hospital. From there she was finally brought home to Sri Lanka by the government. Doctors in Sri Lanka later removed twenty-one nails and other sharp objects from her body. The photographs of the nails stuck in her arms and legs shocked the nation. For a while, Arayawathie was top news. There was even the promise of a government-funded new house. When I spoke with her, about a year after her return and after Rizana's execution, she was despondent and easily irritable.

'I was used by the Saudis and now by the Sri Lankans,' she said. The government did in fact provide her with a house, but that did not mean the family escaped the clutches of dire poverty. Ariyawhathie is still struggling, but at the end of our meeting, she felt grateful. 'I was the lucky one—I could have ended up like Rizana.'

*

Nafeek and Ariyawathie have been the worst cases so far, but periodically, the papers carry reports of other domestic workers returning after physical abuse. Last year, the body of one Sri Lankan domestic worker who had died in Saudi Arabia in late 2015 returned after languishing for almost two-and-a-half-years in a morgue. The woman, who had worked in the kingdom as a maid for over twenty years, had been dumped at the hospital when she fell sick, and no one wanted to claim her body.

Top government officials, like former Foreign Employment Minister Talatha Athokorale, say that Sri Lanka has entered into MoUs with important labour destinations like Saudi Arabia, Qatar and the UAE, enabling better monitoring and protection.

In February 2018, the Sri Lankan mission in the UAE said that women seeking shelter in its premises had dropped to five from a high of thirty, two years ago. Mission officials said that in December 2017 there was not a single Sri Lankan domestic worker seeking shelter in the embassy—the first time this had happened in almost five years.

'People tell me that things are much better now, especially since Rizana's tragedy, but I am sure there are hundreds of cases of suffering,' Ariyawathie said.

No War, No Aid

Some of the latest and worst cases are coming from the Northern region, an area historically not known for migrant labour—that is, until the three-decade-long brutal civil war ended in 2009. The war brought untold tragedies, but it also made sure that the poorest of the poor did not leave the region. Now, migration has increased hugely from this region.

The area, popularly known as the Vanni, is one of the poorest in the island. The 2017 unemployment rate in the province was almost 7.7 per cent, almost twice the national figure of 4.2 per cent. Alarmingly the figure jumps to 15 per cent amongst women in the province, whereas the corresponding national figure is 6 per cent.

The female population in the region is especially vulnerable to economic stagnation. The UN estimates that at least 58,000 of the 250,000 households in the Northern Province are headed by a single female. The war left a large portion of the women between the ages of eighteen and seventy saddled with providing for families, including some with war-disabled members. With grants and aid drying out, these women have found it increasingly difficult to provide for their households, which make up at least one-fifth of the province's population of 1.5 million. They have been lured by job agents and others to migrate as domestic workers within Sri Lanka and outside.

One such person is Nathkulasinham Nesemalhar, a fifty-five-year-old mother of two from the northern town of Jaffna, where she is a member of the country's Tamil minority. After years of struggling to look after two kids, since she lost her husband during the war, it did not take job agents much effort to convince her that the Gulf was the land of promises. Nesemalhar borrowed money, got herself her first passport at the age of fifty-four and, in March 2017, was on a plane heading to Oman, dreaming that all her life's problems were now over.

What transpired in the Gulf state was the beginning of another nightmare for her. Instead of being placed in a middle-class household in the capital, Muscat, as she had been made to expect, she found herself working for a poor household, hours away from the capital. When she complained that her workload was too much, she was locked up in a room. Then strange men from a recruitment agency came and bundled her off to the capital. Despite the harsh treatment there, she hoped that her condition would improve.

Far from it. Nesemalhar next found herself in a room with fifteen other Sri Lankan women of different ages. All of them had been brought there from dissatisfied households and now the recruitment agency was using them as day labourers, sending them off to various sites to do cleaning work.

One of them used a mobile and alerted her family. However, things did not change overnight. There was no end to the cycle of being transported to various offices to work, and there was no official communication from families or the Sri Lankan government. And there was no pay.

But at least one organization in Sri Lanka, the oddly named but intricately networked Association for Friendship and Love (AFRIEL), based in the Northern town of Vavuniya, had gotten wind that four war-widows were among the fifteen women held in Oman.

Ravindra De Silva, who heads AFRIEL, got Sri Lankans in Muscat to track down the group and give them mobile phones. He used this on-the-ground network to quickly figure out that the women had been motivated to seek overseas jobs by local scouts in Sri Lanka. The scouts told him that they were working on behalf of a recruitment agency in Colombo, over 300 kilometres away from Vavuniya, and were paid a sum for each woman who went overseas. 'The way they operate has not changed a bit from the time they located Rizana Nafeek. They look for simple signs: poverty and dependents. The only thing that has changed is that they are now a bit scared to recruit under-aged girls. But there are enough poor women who will fall for the schemes,' De Silva said.

He got in touch with the job agency and was left gobsmacked by their response—the managers told him that the agency had obtained money for the workers sent to Oman, and any repatriation before the agreed terms were fulfilled would entail compensation payments. De Silva was informed that if each of the stranded workers in Oman were to pay 300,000 Sri Lankan rupees (about US$1,900), they could be brought back without delay. The agency was playing both sides: it had taken money from the women—around 200,000 Sri Lankan rupees (about US$1,148) each—to send them overseas, while also charging money from the Omani agency for providing the labourers. Now, it was in a bind when the women left their original workplaces. The Omani agency, in turn, had charged families a fee to provide them domestic workers and had to pay that back. Thus, they were using the women as slaves to earn back their money.

De Silva then got in touch with the Ministry of Foreign Employment and the minister in charge at the time, Athukolrale, intervened to get the women brought back to Sri Lanka. However, she admitted that if the Omani agency had refused to release the women, there would have been very little leverage with the government. 'In this case, we made sure that we brought these women back,' she said. 'If there are other cases like that, we will look at what we can do, but in the majority of cases these women have gone overseas within legally accepted frameworks.'

*

De Silva is certain that the women were sexually abused. He told me that Nesemalhar had hinted at such abuse to female staff members in his office. But she has not said anything to him or to others, on record. After about an hour of talking to her, I asked her if she was physically harmed. Her eyes widened for a second and she stared back momentarily. But she regained her composure and told me that she was slapped once or twice; other than that, there was nothing more. She had not been physically or medically examined on her return.

Local media have also reported that women who travel to the Gulf as migrant workers are being given powerful contraceptives without their knowledge. The injections are administered during medical tests conducted through the job agencies. Reports have identified several women from the North and East who were given the injections without their knowledge or approval. But the agencies make sure that the women sign documents that allow for medical examinations and treatments.

Even without the threat of rape, going overseas for work for women from the Vanni invites stigmatization. Villagers make fun of them and call out that they are prostitutes or whores for Arabs. Even Nesemalhar's children, now in their twenties, have told her that they feel embarrassed that she went to Oman and had to be brought back by the government. 'People think that I worked as a whore,' she said.

Women from the Vanni appeared to have broken out of the traditional stranglehold of patriarchal abuse during the war, when the LTTE formed female armed units and promoted female cadres to equal positions as their male colleagues. However, Nesemalhar says that all that was a façade and, that since the war's end, discrimination has worsened. 'When officers find out that a single woman with children is seeking their assistance, most of the time they ask favours; they will ask you to meet them at various locations and want you to do all kind of things,' she said.

The Vanni is full of stories of both government and NGO officials seeking sexual favours from female beneficiaries. However, there is yet to be a major investigation or conviction. In 2015, the Sri Lankan Red Cross did investigate allegations of sexual misconduct against one of its technical officers in the Vanni. The investigation, based on a beneficiary's complaint, found no evidence to support the claims.

'The thing is that the culture is such here that no one will talk about these things,' says De Silva. He related that in late 2018, public officials banned representatives of micro-finance companies and loan collectors from visiting several villages in the Vavuniya District after dusk, since several had been assaulted by villagers for soliciting sexual favours.

*

In the last three years, only about 3,000 women from the Vanni have sought overseas employment, an insignificant number compared to national figures. But De Silva and others point out that the numbers are increasing. 'Last year we had a case when police arrested a man with over thirty new passports of local women, all looking after families,' he relates. 'The suspicion was he had gotten them in touch with Colombo-based recruitment agencies and was in the process of moving them to Colombo to go overseas.'

The major reason women from the Vanni seek employment is poverty. 'The economic gains are restricted to the major cities in the Vanni, like Jaffna and Vavuniya; there are no significant assistance programmes right now, either by the government or others like the UN—there is no money for that. So, these women have very few options,' explains S. Senthurajah, Executive Director of the Jaffna-based Social Organisations Networking for Development (SOND).

Not surprisingly, when I met her, Nesemalhar was on another, costly mission to escape, as she has been trying to all her life. She was again borrowing money to seek overseas employment. She said that she cannot live in her village because there were all kinds of stories about her, which her two children did not like. On top of all that, she was still several hundred thousand rupees in debt from her last ill-fated attempt to work in the Gulf.

That experience should have deterred her from a second try. 'But what am I to do,' she says. 'If I stay here, there are no jobs, there is no money and I am in debt. If I go overseas at least I will have a job and a chance of paying off the loans.'

This time, she is also in the sights of loan sharks who have demanded that she leave the deed to her land with them. 'If I fail to pay, I lose my land, which is probably ten times more valuable than the loan! I know the dangers, but I also know I have no other option.'

Notes

1. http://www.fao.org/news/story/en/item/897245/icode/

Migrant Journeys

Making the Films

KESANG TSETEN

The making of each film has its own history, specific circumstances and factors shaping the outcome. So it was with the two films I began making in 2007 about Nepali male migrants working in the GCC countries. The first film, titled *In Search of the Riyal,* centred on the stories of four young scaffolders in Nepal and their onward journey to the Gulf. The second, titled *The Desert Eats Us,* captured numerous other stories of migrant lives in Qatar.

The films were eventually screened at international film festivals and venues, across cities like Busan, Paris, Geneva, Leipzig, New York and Delhi; they were also widely screened in Nepal; aired on Nepalese television, supported by Amnesty International; and used by NGOs and others working for the cause of safer migration. Few Nepalis had seen images of these labour destinations then, even though large numbers of their compatriots were already going to these countries and their remittances were keeping the country afloat during the decade-long civil war between Maoist militia and State security forces.

The Early Films

The making of those films in 2008 was conditioned by one overriding factor: the difficulty of access and the dire conditions under which access was possible. The GCC countries are the touchiest on anything that taints their image—and particularly about the armies of migrant workers that have built the gleaming infrastructure for which their cities are known. A pipeline of cheap labour from South Asia, the Philippines, Sudan and other poor countries underpins their lifestyle, but, despite all scrutiny and criticism, the conditions under which migrant workers live and work remain dire.

Given this background, and the low odds of securing a permit, particularly since I was a filmmaker from a poor, labour-sending country, we filmed on the sly. In Qatar, for example, my partner and I filmed for ten days, without even trying to apply for permits to do so, on the assumption that the permits would not have been forthcoming, and the authorities would have been alerted to our intentions. My cameraman and I went in with consumer handi-cams to avoid attention. We took utmost care to film solely in places where only migrant workers went, away from surveillance and CCTV cameras. These constraints became even more acute after Qatar won the bid to host the FIFA 2022 World Cup in 2010, as international attention zoomed in on the 'slave labour' involved in the building of the stadia and related infrastructure.

Despite all the constraints, we could film in many places: the Nepal embassy; Nepalese restaurants that were patronized by migrants for their weekly fill of momos and chow mien; the quiet back alleys and public squares where thousands of migrants congregated on Fridays, their off-day; in labour camps where Nepalis were in charge and could invite us; and in the desert where Nepalis had unwittingly landed up as herders of camels and goats, and as vegetable growers.

We succeeded in our objective, probably because the FIFA bid had not happened yet, nor had the *Guardian*'s reportage and videos highlighting the appalling conditions of migrants in Qatar. Though the working conditions in the Gulf have subsequently come under intense media scrutiny and criticism, they remain largely unchanged, as does the inflow of migrants, propelled by the dismal economic opportunities in their own countries. That is the paradox.

Why These Films?

When I began filming, Nepali labour migration had been going on for about two decades. Over that time, an estimated 2 million Nepalis went abroad.[1] By 2010, remittances made up 17 per cent of the country's GDP, and one in every three Nepali households depended on them.[2] The importance of migration and remittances for Nepal was my primary reason for making this film. The other reason was filmic: I wanted to know how to make a film about a phenomenon of such magnitude, where so many do the same thing for the same reason. Or, to put it differently, documentaries are generally about something unique and singular, and here was a phenomenon that seemed pretty universal; thus, how to find a Story among a glut of similar stories.

This problem was solved by deciding to focus on individual aspiring migrants in a program that targetted poor youth, deprived of a high-school education, for training in carpentry, masonry and scaffolding, so that they might secure better wages when they went abroad. I chose to follow individuals, trying to get a cross-section in terms of ethnicity and caste. I visited their village homes and met two of them again, in Qatar, to where they had been recruited.

What I learned from filming these two works was that, first and importantly, migration is a reality—an undisputable given. You can debate whether migration is good or bad until you're blue in the face, but people continue to migrate. In any case, this is a discussion that the middle class most engage in, exactly the people who do not migrate to these destinations.

The core underlying argument of the first film was that Nepalis went abroad as a rational choice—and who was to say that they were wrong to do so? A filmmaker is often waging a private argument with someone or some idea. For me, it was the notion that people went because they didn't know better; and further, that this was a bad thing, as it drained the country of much-needed manpower. I thought this view lazy and sentimental, in the vein of: 'Oh, wouldn't it be good if everyone stayed home and raised chickens or goats or grew cucumber!' Most times, the person holding such a view would cite an example of someone living such a rural idyll successfully. At worst, I found the discussion patronizing and self-serving: the person would recall their horror upon flying a Qatar or Gulf airline, where they'd witnessed how Nepali migrants would be herded and ill-treated—the source of much shame for them, as one sharing the nationality of the migrants. 'And just for Rs 15,000!' they would exclaim, forgetting that it is anything but easy for most people to earn such a monthly salary (about US$128) in Nepal.

Thus, *In Search of the Riyal* had a lot in it about lives in hinterland Nepal as well as a wide range of stories about workers' conditions in Qatar, narrated by a real character, an activist journalist living there. The film took on a large canvas and was quite political.

The rationale for the second film *The Desert Eats Us* was that it *showed* the lot of the migrants in Qatar. Its underlying argument was that while Nepalis were compelled to go abroad to better their lot, in spite of the risks of being scammed and exploited, it didn't justify their poor treatment in some of the richest countries in the world. It was to point to the fundamentally wrong premise of the arrangement between employer and employee, metropol and satellite.

In both films, it was vital, however, that we understand and sympathize with Nepalis opting to go abroad; above all, to accept their exercise of agency.

Migrant Journeys

A decade later, as a Panos Southasia Fellow, I have the opportunity to revisit the subject of migration through this sequel to my earlier films. There is nostalgia for the experiences of those earlier film projects that provided adventure and discovery for a filmmaker, delving into the lives of a swathe of the Nepali underclass for whom migration seems to be the only beacon. I should mention though, that while much of my filming back then was about migrants in dire, and even desperate circumstances, a significant share of migrant stories were positive and successful. There *have* to be, given that now, in 2017, migrating numbers have reached an estimated 3 million[3], with half of all Nepali males between the ages of eighteen and forty having gone abroad, and remittances having increased to up to 30 per cent of the GDP.[4] Today, migration has grown even more vital for Nepal, both economically and socially.

I've always found it difficult to respond to the question most asked: is migration a good or bad thing? To me, it's like asking, 'Is life good or bad?' Clearly, it depends—it depends on which particular migrant experience out of a few million we look at. A blanket answer is impossible, as a vast number of configurations have to be taken into account. Even if someone were to answer that it is good, what they'd most likely be saying is, 'It's good in this regard, but…' Thus, the perennial answer to that perennial question has to be: 'It depends (stupid)!' More importantly, the clear urgency of seeing how to better facilitate and protect what is an unstoppable tidal wave leaving the country is ignored in favour of this fatuous discussion.

Certainly, there is an argument that large-scale migration creates the trap of economic dependency; neglect of the country's internal manpower and its farms; and an easy adoption of consumerism afforded by remittances; not to speak of the social impact of migration, including family upheaval, a dominant theme of this present film. But it behoves us to acknowledge and appreciate why the phenomenon persists.

Migrant Journeys, the present film, centres on four characters, with little leeway for anything not directly linked to them. Capturing and manifesting character in ways that is strictly related to their theme (migration) is a challenge, but I wanted to do just that for a principal reason: that, too often, the primary motivation for such an exploration is its affective importance to the economy. That is to say, it is driven by instrumentalist aims, at the cost of considering the impact on people. I wanted to place their individual stories centre-stage.

I chose these four, not because they 'represented' the migrant experience, but because their stories offered a longitudinal view— their initial foray, the reasons for it, and the results of that. Thus, where the earlier film was complex and political, the present film has a more intimate canvas. But it looks at their personal lives, giving that equal importance for a change. I was happy to revisit, to encounter this world of varied, complex experiences; to see what has changed; and if I could glean new insights, however minute, into this massive trend. There is a palpable vividness to the migrant story, to how real lives play out in the migrant world that invites engagement from a bystander—for that is who we filmmakers are, at the end of the day. We make a film, which might take a year or two, and then move on.

*

Back in 2008, the four young men were just starting their adult lives. Two were leaving their newly-wed wives, one an infant in a cradle, another a difficult depressive household. All four were from marginalized communities—two were Dalit—for escape and for transformation. How had it all gone for them? How had that venture on which so much rested played out? Where were they today?

It was easy to locate the four characters. **Dhanvir**, I found, is on Facebook, albeit under a different account; he is still in Qatar, with the same company that hired him eleven years earlier. **Prem** had been living not far from the eastern town of Dharan; I had filmed him in Qatar back then, but he seemed to have returned to Nepal after two years. A local journalist found him easily. Prem was in touch with **Bhoj** in nearby Jhapa and passed along his phone number. He, too, spent a year in Dubai and then a year in Qatar but had returned home because of family. Only **Nabin Rai**'s whereabouts were hard to trace; I'd visited him at his village near Gaighat, just as I'd visited all the others in their villages in 2008–2009. There was only one way to find him, which was to go to his village.

I made a plan to track Nabin from his village, and to meet Prem and Bhoj after that. I flew to Biratnagar, then hired a Scorpio, the ubiquitous rough-road vehicle for mountainous and flat Nepal. The sparse settlements in the eastern Nepal foothills were denser than before: more settlements and more people. After asking many people, describing the family and the location as I remembered it (near a small school, on the outskirts of Gaighat, the district headquarters), we soon located the lane, then the gravel road leading to Nabin's parents' farmhouse amidst a thicket of trees. His father instantly recognized me and told me that Nabin was abroad. For some reason, I'd assumed Nabin might have been doing carpentry or house-painting in the nearby town—perhaps I'd heard at some point that he'd returned from a stint in the Gulf. His father, a big man in his mid-sixties, told me that Nabin had visited a few months earlier. 'He comes often to finish that,' he said, pointing to a house still being built, with reinforced iron rods protruding above the flat cement roof. 'But it's taking time to do it,' he added, with a laugh.

I learned that Nabin had initially gone abroad for two years; he hadn't liked the work or the company, and had returned to do carpentry and construction work. When he got another job and a free visa to go abroad again, he had grabbed the opportunity. Nabin's father explained, 'He was getting decent pay, sometimes even a thousand rupees a day, but there'd be work for ten days and then no work for fifteen days. So, he went back abroad. And he's still there, now at a gas plant. I think he gets a good salary and he gets to come home every three months.' Then he told me, as most village Nepalis are forthcoming about their private lives, 'But he and his wife have separated. She took off with a guy from Darjeeling,' he said, with a chuckle, which often accompanies the disclosing of sensitive information by such Nepalis. He elaborated. 'What to do? She left the twins, two girls, said, "take them", and took off.' He continued, 'I told him he shouldn't think of trying to get his money back from her—he had just sent a few lakh rupees. I told him, "She's given you children! What more do you want? Let her go her own way!"' The last part was said with a hint of anger.

Back in 2009, they'd been newly-weds, married just before he left for the Gulf. There's a wonderful romantic shot of the two coming out of church, he in a crisp white shirt, she under a blue umbrella, when he had said, 'It's sad to leave. The Bible says we need a year together to let the relationship grow.' They were both Christian.

Two years ago, he had married again, a school teacher. I met her as she returned from school with the twins on cycles. She said that Nabin came home from Dubai as frequently as every three months as he was now a foreman. Thus, separation was not so difficult. In fact, she said, she preferred he come less often so that money could be saved towards finishing the house.

Nabin got in touch with me on Facebook a day later. I knew that getting a visa for Dubai would be difficult, but perhaps it would be easier to get a single-day transit visa on my way back from Europe to meet him. Nabin said he never knew in advance when he would come to shore, and whether his shore-leave would coincide with my stopover, but that he was headed to Kathmandu soon. I was sure I would go to meet him in his village when he came home, but I wanted to have some footage of Nabin outside Nepal. After all, this was a film about Nabin being abroad. How could I shoot everything within Nepal?

Then I discovered that Nabin was flying to Kathmandu on exactly the same day I was returning from a film festival in London. I got him to agree to fly back on the same flight, saying I would cover any extra cost. And so it was that I met Nabin in Abu Dhabi airport, and then on the flight, where I filmed our conversation. Filming without permits, as I did in Doha back in 2008, and with Nabin last year, is increasingly risky. The authorities and police tend to catch everyone who does it, but they would never grant a filming permit to someone from a labour-sending country.

Nabin's migrant experience was somewhat like **Dhanvir Jogi's**, the other one still working abroad, in Qatar. It was fairly straightforward to secure a visa after I invited my journalist protagonist of the earlier film, Devendra Bhattarai, to go with me. He had worked in Doha for several years and is a superb journalist with friends in Qatar. He was knowledgeable about the way things worked there and I knew he would open doors for me—which he did, by getting me a visa through a friend who was a travel agent.

That first morning in Doha, a Friday and thus a holiday, we met Dhanvir. The first thing I'd noticed about him when I met him eleven years ago, soon after he settled in Qatar, was how much weight he had put on, compared to the lean youth from Terhathum he'd been at the training centre. He himself had seemed baffled about it, and had speculated that it was the food in Qatar, which is frozen and loaded with chemicals to keep it unspoiled for a long period.

Eleven years later, Dhanvir is with the same construction company where he began. His monthly salary was US$200–250 then, and he now earns US$1,000 as a foreman scaffolder. In the earlier film, Dhanvir came across as a successful migrant. In a scene in that film of his workplace, his co-workers say how good it is to be in a place where one can meet Nepalis from all seventy-five districts, and he shows off his yellow scaffolding outfit.

Today, he recounts that his initial ambition coming here was to make one hundred thousand Nepali rupees, then two, then three, so he that he can 'run a teashop and be happy', as he put it. His objective had changed, almost without his being aware of it, and a decade later, he was still here. He took us to his camp in the desert, from where he and his team commute daily to work on one segment of the Doha metro extension. We would also film him on a visit to his temporary rented home in Dhankuta, with his wife and his eleven-year-old son.

Poignantly, the old film has a shot of his son as an infant in a cradle swinging to and fro on the eve of Dhanvir's departure for the Gulf. His deep regret about his long tenure in the Gulf is that he missed watching his son grow up. The first time he saw his son on home leave from Qatar, his son was more than two years old. That day, his son called Dhanvir 'Daddy' for the first time, overwhelming him with emotion. He reflected that it was because he had missed out on carrying the boy during those tender first few months of his life. During his visit this time, Dhanvir seemed very much the father wanting to make up for time lost. He took his son to school, fetched him at day's end; discussed homework and goings-on at school with him. Because of his father-in-law's recent death, his wife was absent for thirteen days of mourning, and so we captured Dhanvir in close interaction with his son.

Dhanvir says he will probably work until he's somewhere between thirty-five and forty years old—he is thirty-three now. He cites a popular Nepali song that prescribes forty to be the age when a man should retire and enjoy life. For the time being, he believes he must continue working abroad, to support his family and his parents, and most of all, to ensure his son gets the best education possible.

Prem Bareilly lives in the same settlement at the outskirts of Dharan that I visited back when I was making *In Search of the Riyal*. Following his training in 2008, he went to Doha to work for a Chinese company. They did not pay on time, and mistreated him, including hitting him. He blamed the lack of a common language with his employers for the difficulties he experienced. On top of all that, the employer did not allow Prem to return home every two years, which is the norm. So he quit and returned to Nepal, something he often regrets.

Even today, Prem takes pride in his abilities (winning 'worker of the month' once) as a migrant worker. He had always spoken of difficulties at home: a father who was depressive; the tragedy of a sister who committed suicide during a festival; his family's unfortunate former village where, most probably as Dalits, they lived on a steeply sloping piece of farmland, subject to marauding wild animals. A massive landslide destroyed his home, killing several relatives, and forcing the family to seek new land on which to settle. That summed up his despair and his family's marginalization, both economically and as Dalit, which he, as the only son, was expected to overcome.

On his return from Qatar, he took up his caste trade as a silversmith. He rents a bare room in the village centre that he calls his shop, his business. Unfortunately, people from other castes have encroached into his traditional occupation, thereby intensifying competition. He said he can make ends meet, but saving is impossible, and so the future is bleak. He supports his immediate family, including his parents. Consequently, he has no choice but to contemplate going abroad again, though his parents are against that.

When the protagonists have a reunion, Prem asks Nabin to help him, by alerting him when his company puts a call out for recruits. Nabin says he cannot promise that, as he himself might not know about it when it happens. Prem presses the issue. Nabin explains that the demand for scaffolding has diminished, and the salary is low. Prem takes this as Nabin's being reluctant to help him. He argues that scaffolding remains a tough occupation, and that he can cope with any degree of difficulty and risk. He says that his wife agrees that making silver jewellery will not bring them a secure future, and is pushing him to go abroad.

Bhojraj Darzi, from Jhapa, had short stints in Dubai and Qatar. First, he'd been deported from Dubai for striking, though it was the other workers who had framed him. The second time, in Qatar, he'd got a well-paying job at the airport. But just as all was going well, his wife fell very ill, and Bhoj was forced to leave the Gulf. On his return home, he'd taken up his caste profession, tailoring, and helped the domestic weaving his mother had started many years back. It was doing well. But, his brother, who had started a business in livestock, died in a freak accident. Since the business was lucrative, Bhojraj decided to take it over. Three days a week, he and his partner drove their minivan to comb villages around Jhapa for piglets, which they procured, collected, and took to the famous Dharan pig market to sell every Friday.

I visited Bhoj at his large family farmhouse crowded with looms and weavers in the middle of paddy fields. He was in between his pig-buying jaunts. We exchanged the usual 'You've put on weight' remarks, after which he recounted his personal history over the past eleven years. He had never seen the film in which he was a protagonist, so I happily showed it on my laptop. He, his family and the weavers watched, with excitement, the scenes in which Bhoj figures.

Bhoj seemed settled and contented. The weaving business his mother started twenty-five years ago was thriving, and the pig business represented a step-up in entrepreneurship. Later, at the protoganists' get-together, he spoke of how lucrative the business was, declaring that he would continue it life long.

Since each of the group was curious about the others and were all from the east, we decided on a get-together in Dharan. Unfortunately for the reunion (more importantly, for the film!), an unexpected vehicle strike blocking mobility in and from nearby Dhankuta, as well as the death of his father-in-law prevented Dhanvir from attending. Without any prodding, the remaining three discussed and exchanged experiences, recalling the time they had met each other in Kathmandu. Time and again, what makes filming Nepalis such a pleasure is their open natures; intuitively they help the process, without making any gratuitous gestures.

*

What to include and what to eliminate is obviously most crucial in a documentary. The hybrid form of the documentary allows immense malleability; at the end, you can do anything that works. While editing, I decided to chuck many things that were in the original plan. For instance, there were six key characters, not four, in *In Search of the Riyal.* One of them, whose story I'd included in the earlier film, went out for the simple reason that he was never recruited to go abroad. Taking out the other person was a bigger decision. He was older, and not part of the training scheme, but someone who had figured prominently in the earlier film. I'd met him in Dubai during an early research trip.

This was **Dalbir Bareilly**, an ex-Nepal army man, who'd been in the UAE for several years when I met him. He returned to Nepal following the breakup of his marriage, which he attributed to distance and separation from his wife. He remarried, and not wanting to repeat his mistakes, had looked for work in Nepal. By coincidence, he found a job with the NGO (F-Skill) that had provided training to the four young scaffolders. Because of his long migrant experience, he'd been hired to counsel would-be migrants on psycho-social issues and to rehearse them through the emotional facets of migration.

Dalbir's story made up the last part of the earlier film *In Search of the Riyal*, which was divided into GOING, BEING THERE and RETURNING, to illustrate the cycle of migration. This last section illustrates the situation whereby a migrant's economic gains sustain and create opportunities for his family, but which force him to continue the cycle in order to maintain these opportunities. And true to type, Dalbir left the counselling job to return to being a security guard in the UAE some months later. For him, not doing so would have undone all his gains. His was a common predicament.

As I had not been able to get a visa for Dubai for the real filming, I filmed him and his family in their Kathmandu apartment, to which they had moved from their village in Ramechap. His ageing mother now has access to better medical facilities; his daughter, whom I'd captured as a young child, was attending college; and his son was in the UK, studying accountancy. As the film developed, clearly, his story did not fit. He had little in common with the four young scaffolders, whose birth, for the purposes of this film, had started with their shared experiences of moving from the training centre to their first jobs abroad.

*

I don't believe film is the ideal medium to transmit knowledge. What it can do well is excavate meaning and make it come alive through stories. The individual lives presented in these films chronicle Nepali migrant experiences that illuminate, and perhaps instruct, via *stories*, the complexity of not just migrant but all Nepali lives.

There's no 'average' or 'representative' story that stands for all, though it's natural to seek such conclusive meanings—it makes life easier. This is the predilection that afflicts the profession and class that talks, writes and reflects, and in this case, makes films about others' meanings. And because it is about 'others,' we tend to seek answers and knowledge that is expedient or instrumentalist. We, the 'knowledge-producing' class, prefer definite, conclusive answers to big questions, rather than: 'It depends.' The search for knowledge and meaning, is itself inevitably inflected: 'For whom? For what?'

Given migration's significance in Nepal's society, such *public* representations are not only useful but essential. As has been said, *experience is experience reflected*: migration needs to be reflected and experienced among the larger society as a precondition to— and as going hand in hand with—successful civil society, NGO and governmental initiatives.

Notes

1. https://esa.un.org/miggmgprofiles/indicators/files/Nepal.pdf
2. https://www.mdpi.com/2227-7099/5/2/16/pdf-vor
3. https://esa.un.org/miggmgprofiles/indicators/files/Nepal.pdf
4. https://www.mdpi.com/2227-7099/5/2/16/pdf-vor

About the Authors

Haniya Javed is from Karachi, Pakistan, where she has been working as a reporter for *Express Tribune* (an English daily working in partnership with *New York Times*). She covered NGOs, minorities, human rights, social injustice and arts and culture for two years in Karachi. She has a Masters degree from Columbia Journalism School where she honed her reporting in investigative skills, data journalism and audience engagement. (haniyajaved1@gmail.com)

Upasana Khadka is a freelancer associated with the *Nepali Times*. She has written pieces on migration, internally displaced people and social justice (http://upasanakhadka.portfoliobox.net/). Upasana has also worked on international migration issues with the Ministry of Labor, Employment and Social Security in Nepal and the World Bank in Washington DC. She holds a Master's degree in Public Administration and International Development (MPA/ID) from the Harvard Kennedy School of Government, and an interdisciplinary degree in Economics and Mathematics from Reed College, USA. She is interested in writing, data analysis and photography. (u.khadka@gmail.com)

Upasana would like to thank her journalism mentor and editor, Kunda Dixit, for his inspiration and guidance. She is also grateful to her parents, Rup and Anita, and her brother, Utsab, for their unwavering support and to the Panos family for the laughter and camaraderie.

Nila Kumar is a freelance journalist based in India.

Rejimon Kuttappan is a Senior India-Arab Gulf Investigator with Equidem Research and Consulting probing migrant workers' rights. Headquartered in the UK, Equidem is a specialist human rights and labour rights consultancy dedicated to defending the human rights of vulnerable individuals and communities, including migrant workers, women, children and minorities, in the context of labour migration and humanitarian and post-conflict settings.

He is an advisor for the Ethical Journalism Network Labour Migration Fellowship and, as a journalist, has reported on migration for Thomson Reuters Foundation, *Equal Times, Migrant Rights, Middle East Eye, The Caravan, The Wire, Scroll.in, Vice India* and various Indian news portals. He was deported by the Oman government in April 2017, following his reports in the *Times of Oman* on human trafficking of migrant workers in Oman. (reji.news@gmail.com)

Thulasi Muttulingam is a freelance journalist based in the post-war region of Jaffna, Sri Lanka, reporting on post-war developments there. She is an alumna of the Sri Lanka College of Journalism, as well as the Asian College of Journalism in India. She has been the recipient of several prestigious international fellowships and grants from around the world, including the Chevening Journalism Fellowship (UK) and International Visitor Leadership Program (USA). She also does outreach work via social media to take the fruits of her research work to the masses. She is the founder of Humans of Northern Sri Lanka, a popular Facebook page that raises awareness about social realities in that region. She focuses on covering social issues related to war and post-war developments in north and east Sri Lanka. Migration, both internal displacements and exodus abroad, is a key aspect of her writing. (thulasi108@gmail.com)

Porimol Palma is a senior correspondent at *The Daily Star*, the highest-circulated English newspaper in Bangladesh. Journalism is a passion for Porimol who started his career as a cub reporter at a teen magazine. Through his stories, he aspires to influence national, regional and global policies to establish human rights, democracy and pluralism. He has a Masters degree in Development Studies from BRAC University and has worked as a correspondent for Bangkok-based UCANEWS.COM and Philippines-based Radio Veritas Asia. He covers labour migration, human trafficking, agriculture, food safety and health. (porimol25@yahoo.com)

Amantha Perera is a writer and media development strategist based in Colombo, Sri Lanka. His work has appeared in *TIME Magazine*, *The Guardian*, Reuters, *Washington Post, al-Jazeera* and other outlets. He has worked extensively on building awareness on trauma impact and journalism and currently serves as the regional coordinator for Asia-Pacific for the DART Center for Journalism and Trauma, Columbia University. His current research focuses on the trauma impact and the on-line footprint of journalists. He was an International Visiting Scholar at the Graduate School of Journalism, University of California, Berkeley, California. (Twitter: @AmanthaP Email: amantha_23@yahoo.com)

R.K. Radhakrishnan is associate editor of India's *Frontline* magazine. Before moving to *Frontline*, he was with *The Hindu* newspaper for two decades. He served as the paper's bureau chief in Chennai and Tamil Nadu, in the political bureau, and wrote editorials. In 2010, he covered Sri Lanka as the island nation struggled to find peace after its three-decade-old debilitating ethnic conflict. Concurrently, he covered Maldives which saw a series of defining changes from 2012, including a bloodless coup.

Radhakrishnan is adjunct faculty at the Asian College of Journalism, Chennai, and visiting faculty at The Banyan Academy of Leadership in Mental Health, also in the city. He is a regular contributor to the dialogues at India's widely-respected think tank, The Hindu Centre for Politics and Public Policy, and writes on a range of issues related to Indian polity for it. (radha9110@gmail.com)

Janak Raj Sapkota is a journalist and social researcher associated with Nepal's largest daily newspaper, *Kantipur Publications*. His academic and journalistic interests are focused on sustained research and coverage of issues pertaining to labour migration and mobility. His first book *Kahar: Baideshik rojgarile bitholindo samaj* (2016) talks about how Nepali society was disordered by labour migration and the social impacts of remittances. A short documentary based on book can be seen here: https://www.youtube.com/watch?v=QPp-4auvgBQ). He then co-authored a book based on qualitative research, *The Social Impact of Remittance in Terai*. His most recent book, *Dukha dekhi dukha samma* (2018) covers an in-depth analysis of migration in selected Nepali novels published over the last eighty years. (janaksapkota048@gmail.com)

Sabrina Toppa is an independent journalist based in Pakistan, whose work has appeared in *The Guardian, The Atlantic, TIME Magazine, The Washington Post*, Public Radio International, and *Al Jazeera* English, among other outlets. She previously worked in the offices of *Mother Jones* in San Francisco, *TIME Magazine* in Hong Kong, *The Dhaka Tribune*, and *The Kathmandu Post*. Sabrina is a 2018 Pulitzer Center on Crisis Reporting grantee, covering the impact of Chinese investment in Pakistan. Her reporting on child marriage in Pakistan won the 2018 Humanitarian Reporting Award from the International Committee of the Red Cross and Center for Excellence in Journalism.

Kesang Tseten's documentaries have been regularly screened in Nepal and in international film festivals, including the International Documentary Film Festival of Amsterdam, Leipzig International Documentary Festival, Yamagata, Thessaloniki, Krakow, Viennale and the Margaret Mead Film festival. He has been the recipient of grants from Busan, IDFA and the Sundance Institute for his films. Before filmmaking, Kesang wrote and edited and was associate editor of *Himal Magazine* in its early years. He is a graduate of Dr Graham's School in India and Amherst College and Columbia University in the US. His documentaries on Nepali migrant workers in the Gulf have been screened at various festivals worldwide. (shunyatafilm@gmail.com)

Acknowledgements

The fellowship programme at Panos is a tried and tested method that incorporates a stringent screening process to select fellowship recipients, and close mentoring and monitoring by expert panels for the duration of the fellowship. Ramyata Limbu, the project director for this fellowship programme, and Rati Sharma, the finance manager were instrumental for its timely and efficient implementation.

Lakshmi Nair, the monitoring and evaluation manager for this programme, kept an eye on the impact generated by every report filed by the fellows. Ujjwal Acharya, the web editor at PSA, ensured that all journalistic outputs were listed in the Labour Migration blog on Panos South Asia's web portal and got effective traction on social media platforms. The ILO, country office Nepal, and the Ethnical Journalism Network have been active supporters of this fellowship programme.

Many years ago, Sir Harold Evans called sub-editors the hidden impresarios of news. Shalini Krishan of our publisher, Speaking Tiger, is the hidden impresario of this anthology. She took pride in translating the complex into the comprehensible, in making sense of conflicting information from divergent sources, and forcing the fellows to revise their copy till it managed to acquire a self-sustaining glow.